Children of God

Children of God
A Musical

by Corey Payette
(book/music/lyrics)

Children of God
first published 2018 by Scirocco Drama
An imprint of J. Gordon Shillingford Publishing Inc.
© 2018 Corey Payette

Scirocco Drama Editor: Glenda MacFarlane
Cover design by Terry Gallagher/Doowah Design
Cover photo by Matt Barnes, Model: Michelle Bardach
Author photo by Nadya Kwandibens
Production photos by Emily Cooper Photography
Disclaimer: This is a work of fiction: names, characters, places, and events
are the product of the playwright's imagination, or are used fictitiously.
Any resemblance to actual persons living or dead, or to events or locales,
is entirely coincidental.

Printed and bound in Canada on 100% post-consumer recycled paper.
We acknowledge the financial support of the Manitoba Arts Council and
The Canada Council for the Arts for our publishing program.

Production inquiries should be addressed to:
Playwrights Guild of Canada
401 Richmond Street West, Suite 350
Toronto, Ontario
M5V 3A8
416-703-0201
info@playwrightsguild.ca

Library and Archives Canada Cataloguing in Publication

Payette, Corey, 1987-, author
    Children of God / a musical by Corey Payette (book/music/lyrics).

A play.
ISBN 978-1-927922-38-5 (softcover)

1. Indians of North America--Ontario, Northern--Drama. I. Title.

PS8631.A932C55 2018   C812'.6   C2017-907380-X

J. Gordon Shillingford Publishing
P.O. Box 86, RPO Corydon Avenue, Winnipeg, MB Canada R3M 3S3

For Cathy

Corey Payette

Corey Payette is proud of his Oji-Cree heritage from Northern Ontario and has worked as a playwright, actor, composer, and director across Canada. He is the Artistic Director of Urban Ink Productions (Vancouver, BC), was the 2014-15 Artist-in-Residence with English Theatre at Canada's National Arts Centre, and the founder of Raven Theatre (Vancouver, BC) focusing on new works by Indigenous artists. Corey has worked as an Artistic Associate with The Indigenous Cycle at the National Arts Centre, an investigation into the broad spectrum of the Indigenous body of work being created within Canada's borders. This cycle resulted in the creation of a new department of Indigenous Theatre at the National Arts Centre which will begin in 2019.

As a playwright, Corey's work has been developed at the Vancouver Playhouse, Firehall Arts Centre, Western Canada Theatre, Arts Club Theatre, Urban Ink Productions, Full Circle: First Nations Performance, and Raven Theatre. He's currently writing a new musical, *Les Filles du Roi* (music and direction, co-book/lyrics with Julie McIsaac) in English, French, and Kanien'kéha (Mohawk), commissioned by Fugue Theatre.

The album recording *Corey Payette – The Music of Children of God* and the Piano/Vocal songbook are available at www.coreypayette.com

Acknowledgements

Marshall McMahen, Dawn Brennan, Allison Grant, Gloria May Eshkibok, Jillian Keiley, Julie McIsaac, Sarah Garton Stanley, Nathan Medd, Andy Lunney, Heather Redfern, Daryl Cloran, Lori Marchand, Heather Cant, Kate Declerck, Sol Diana, Patrice Bowler, Reneltta Arluk, Kwasuun Sarah Vedan, Lisa, Krystal and Guy Payette, Lindsay Drummond, Jennifer Lines, Arlie Worthing, Michelle Bardach, Micheal Querin, Quelemia Sparrow, Josue Laboucane, Lance Cardinal, Andrew Wheeler, Lauren Bowler, Katey Wright, Renae Morriseau, Ronnie Dean Harris, Margo Kane, Marie Clements, Tanja Dixon-Warren, Rachel Ditor, Bill Millerd, Donna Spencer, Robert McQueen, Max Reimer, Meredith Elliott, Chelsea McPeake Carlton, Julia Mackey, Steven Charles, Sean Bayntun, Clara Shandler, Steven Greenfield, Wes Nahanee, Bob Baker, Jordan Chin, Matt Barnes, Andrea Tétrault, Tanyss Knowles, Sarah Rush, Elizabeth Jones, Indian Residential School Survivors Society, Kamila Sediego, Stephen Courtenay, Jan Hodgson, Ivor McMahen and the National Centre for Truth and Reconciliation.

Playwright Notes

When I was growing up in Northern Ontario, we were never taught the history of residential schools. It wasn't something people talked about. When I learned of this history I felt I needed to do something about it and make sure that people knew what had happened. *Children of God* was born out of anger and frustration that this horrible history had happened and yet was hidden from the narrative of our country.

The journey led me through years of research, speaking with survivors on the back of their pick-up trucks in rural BC, visiting abandoned school sites, and holding a workshop production at the Chief Louis Cultural Centre, a reclaimed former residential school on the Tk'emlúps te Secwèpemc in Kamloops, BC. Every step of this journey changed my outlook as a person, allowed me to have a deeper understanding of the history, and led me to recognize my responsibility in acknowledging the strength and resilience of residential school survivors and their descendants. Over the past seven years, I have witnessed people across the whole country expand their awareness. Through the work of the Truth and Reconciliation Commission, Canadians now have a better understanding of this history; it has gone from something that wasn't talked about to something that we discuss regularly. I believe that for true reconciliation, it can't just be Indigenous peoples who bear the burden of this work. It needs to be everyone, in every community, investing in this process and continuing the journey forward together.

Through this work, we honour and acknowledge the strength of survivors and their descendants. We are proud of Indigenous peoples' resilience in reclaiming our culture, language, and rightful place at the heart of our Canadian identity. Stories are powerful. They connect us, shape our understanding of ourselves and our relationship to one another, so that the true history of this country can be fully understood. Miigwetch (thank you) to the remarkable company of artists who brought *Children of God* to life. And to you, for including this work as a step on our journey to reconciliation.

All my relations,
Corey Payette, 2017
Artistic Director of Urban Ink,
Director, Playwright, Composer, & Lyricist of *Children of God*

Foreword

Facing it.

For the first forty-three years of my life I accepted what I'd been told about my relationship as a settler Canadian to the Indigenous people of this land. And I hadn't been told very much. But I wasn't asking a lot of questions either. I think a lot of us were not asking a lot of questions, together.

. I think I know why.

It is very uncomfortable to face a truth that has been rationalized and ignored and sitting in front of you for years. It severs your tether to your basic beliefs in the good of your country, your religion and your ancestors. It's hard to acknowledge the privilege of a family history that was not systematically riddled with unspeakable abuses, or to recognize that one culture was permitted to thrive while another was suffocated. It's scary to admit that the Canada I love came at a brutal and unnecessary cost to other Canadians.

I believe that many people in my audience at the National Arts Centre (NAC) have had similar reckonings since the Truth and Reconciliation Commission report came to light.

When I first heard of Corey's ambition to work the tragedy of Canadian residential schools into a contemporary musical, I was unconvinced of the idea. I knew he was working diligently at it, even here in an office at the NAC for a while. It seemed like an artistic and social stretch to me, and a politically risky one at that. But Corey never stopped believing in the possibility of using musical theatre to tell the story, honing it and detailing it over and over, draft after draft, equal parts wild inspiration and careful respect.

Finally, I heard pieces from *Children of God* at an NAC gathering of Indigenous performers and creators at the Debajehmujig Creation Centre on Manitoulin Island. I was so deeply moved by it that I kicked myself for having had any doubt. Corey's modern musical take on Canada's most shameful chapter didn't create dissonance between style and subject – it was beautiful and brutal and necessary. It was a way into the story for our audience; an audience that included many who were grappling with the same uncomfortable realizations from the Truth and Reconciliation Commission report that I was, and still am.

In the clear light of history, the abusers and abused are plain to see, but Corey doesn't cheat his audience out of a layered and humane portrayal of all of the characters, no matter what side of history they were on. The music is complex and accessible: by turns wistful, strident, and finally fierce and full of resolution. The denouement of the entire play galvanizes the audience towards reconciliation in a masterstroke of direction, writing, music and spirit the likes of which I have never seen before or since. I cannot tell you how profound it was to see our sophisticated, educated audience reach across the aisles to take one another's hands as the cast and crew willed this communion. They grasped each other in tribute to the families who were devastated, in mourning for the children who were lost, in acknowledgement of the Indigenous women who are still murdered and missing, and in recognition of the commitment and strength it will take for us to face what happened and to begin to move forward, together.

Jillian Keiley
Artistic Director,
English Theatre at Canada's National Arts Centre

Production History

Children of God had its world premiere on May 19ᵗʰ, 2017 at the York Theatre in Vancouver, followed by a run at the National Arts Centre English Theatre in Ottawa.

Produced by Urban Ink (Vancover, BC) in collaboration with the National Arts Centre English Theatre, in association with Raven Theatre (Vancouver, BC). Presented by The Cultch (Vancouver, BC) and Canada Scene (Ottawa, ON).

Original Cast:

TOMMY / TOM ....Herbie Barnes
RITA.. Cathy Elliott
JULIA.. Cheyenne Scott
WILSON SEKORA........................... Kevin Loring
VINCENT SEKORA...................... Aaron M. Wells
JOANNA / SECRETARY......................Kim Harvey
ELIZABETH.......................................Kaitlyn Yott
SISTER BERNADETTE .... Trish Lindström
FATHER CHRISTOPHER .... Michael Torontow

Musicians:
Brian Chan – Cello
Allen Cole – Piano
Martin Reisle – Guitar
Elliot Vaughan – Viola

Creative Team:
Corey Payette – Director / Playwright / Composer / Lyricist
Marshall McMahen – Production Designer
Allen Cole – Musical Director / Piano
Elliot Vaughan – Orchestrator / Viola
Jeff Harrison – Lighting Designer
Reas Calvert – Movement Director

Kris Boyd – Sound Designer
Sybille Pearson – Dramaturg
Julie McIsaac – Associate Director
Helen Oro – Jewelry Design
Mike Kovac & Ryan McNeil Bolton – Fight Directors
Samira Rose – Stage Manager
Jessica Schacht – Assistant Stage Manager

Production Team:
Dawn Brennan – Managing Director
Christie Watson – Producer
Adrian Muir – Production Manager
Darryl Milot – Head of Wardrobe
Carol Macdonald – Props Master
Kyra Soko – Sound Operator

In 2015, *Children of God* received a workshop production in Kamloops at the Chief Louis Cultural Centre (a former residential school.) The show was staged in the chapel of the school and presented "open door" to the community and those who worked at the Cultural Centre. It also had three public performances as part of the High Wire Festival at Western Canada Theatre in Kamloops, BC with the following cast and creative team:

TOMMY/TOM .... Herbie Barnes
RITA.. Cathy Elliott
JULIA .... Michelle Bardach
WILSON SEKORA .... Raes Calvert
VINCENT SEKORA .... Aaron M. Wells
JOANNA/SECRETARY .... Kim Harvey
ELIZABETH................................... Arlie Worthing
SISTER BERNADETTE .... Jennifer Lines
FATHER CHRISTOPHER .... Micheal Querin

Creative Team:
Corey Payette – Director/Playwright/Composer/Lyricist
Marshall McMahen – Production Designer
Julie McIsaac – Musical Director & Assistant Director
Brittany Ryan – Production Design assistant
Elliot Vaughan – Orchestration and Viola
Sybille Pearson – Dramaturg

In 2014, *Children of God* received a reading as part of Arts Club Theatre's ReAct Festival in Vancouver, BC with the following cast and creative team:

TOMMY / TOM ....Josue Laboucane
RITA...Margo Kane
JULIA..Arlie Worthing
WILSON SEKORA...........................Kevin Loring
VINCENT SEKORA......................Aaron M. Wells
JOANNA / SECRETARY......................Kim Harvey
ELIZABETH........................... Quelemia Sparrow
SISTER BERNADETTE ....Jennifer Lines
FATHER CHRISTOPHER ....Micheal Querin

Creative Team:
Corey Payette – Playwright / Composer / Lyricist
Allison Grant – Director
Steven Greenfield – Musical Director
Sybille Pearson – Dramaturg

Workshops were held in previous years through Raven Theatre, Full Circle: First Nations Performance, Firehall Arts Centre, Western Canada Theatre, Vancouver Playhouse, and Sunset Theatre with the following actors and creative team members:

Allison Grant, Gloria May Eshkibok, Sera-lys McArthur, Kevin Loring, Michelle Bardach, Ronnie Dean Harris, Renae Morrisseau, Steven Greenfield, Elliot Vaughan, Lindsay Drummond, Josue Laboucane, Lance Cardinal, Katey Wright, Lauren Bowler, Andrew Wheeler, Patrice Bowler, Sue Newman, and Marshall McMahen.

Actors Herbie Barnes, Kim Harvey, Cheyenne Scott, Kevin Loring, Kaitlyn Yott, and Aaron Wells. An Urban Ink production in association with National Arts Centre English Theatre and Raven Theatre. Production Design by Marshall McMahen, Lighting Design by Jeff Harrison.

Actors Kaitlyn Yott, Herbie Barnes, Aaron Wells, Kim Harvey, Kevin Loring, and Cathy Elliott. An Urban Ink production in association with National Arts Centre English Theatre and Raven Theatre. Production Design by Marshall McMahen, Lighting Design by Jeff Harrison.

Actors Herbie Barnes and Kevin Loring. An Urban Ink production in association with National Arts Centre English Theatre and Raven Theatre. Production Design by Marshall McMahen, Lighting Design by Jeff Harrison.

Actors Michael Torontow, Aaron Wells, Kevin Loring, and Herbie Barnes. An Urban Ink production in association with National Arts Centre English Theatre and Raven Theatre. Production Design by Marshall McMahen, Lighting Design by Jeff Harrison.

Actors Herbie Barnes and Cathy Elliott. An Urban Ink production in association with National Arts Centre English Theatre and Raven Theatre. Production Design by Marshall McMahen, Lighting Design by Jeff Harrison.

Actors Cheyenne Scott and Trish Lindström. An Urban Ink production in association with National Arts Centre English Theatre and Raven Theatre. Production Design by Marshall McMahen, Lighting Design by Jeff Harrison.

Actors Cheyenne Scott and Trish Lindström. An Urban Ink production in association with National Arts Centre English Theatre and Raven Theatre. Production Design by Marshall McMahen, Lighting Design by Jeff Harrison.

Actors Kaitlyn Yott, Cheyenne Scott, Herbie Barnes, Aaron Wells, and Kevin Loring. An Urban Ink production in association with National Arts Centre English Theatre and Raven Theatre. Production Design by Marshall McMahen, Lighting Design by Jeff Harrison.

World Premiere Opening Night photo taken on May 17, 2017. Left to right: Dawn Brennan, Corey Payette, Marshall McMahen, Michael Torontow, Samira Rose, Kevin Loring, Darryl Milot, Brian Chan, Aaron M. Wells, Martin Reisle, Cathy Elliot, Allen Cole, Herbie Barnes, Elliot Vaughan, Cheyenne Scott, Kim Harvey, Adrian Muir, Jeff Harrison, Jessica Schacht, Kaitlyn Yott, Julie McIsaac, Kris Boyd, Kyra Soko, Trish Lindström, Christie Watson, Raes Calvert, Kamila Sediego.

Characters

1950

TOMMY .... A 13-year-old student.
Julia's brother.

JULIA .... A 14-year-old student, a "runner."
Tommy's sister.

WILSON SEKORA .... A 16-year-old student,
Vincent's brother.

VINCENT SEKORA .... A 14-year-old student,
Wilson's brother.

JOANNA .... A 14-year-old student.

ELIZABETH .... A 14-year-old student.

SISTER BERNADETTE .... Head nun, French-Canadian and
in charge of Girls' Dorm.

FATHER CHRISTOPHER ... Head priest, in charge of Boys' Dorm.

1970

TOM .... 33 years old and unemployed, living
on his mother Rita's couch after
being thrown out of his house.

RITA .... Tom and Julia's mother.

WILSON SEKORA .... 36 years old. Manager of national
shipping company.

SECRETARY .... At Wilson's office.

TOMMY/TOM, WILSON, & JOANNA/SECRETARY: *same actor
plays both parts in different time periods.*

Song List

GOD ONLY KNOWS
Full Company

YOUR FATHER
Rita

PATER NOSTER
All Students and Teachers

THE CLOSEST THING TO HOME
Tommy and Julia

WHAT DO THEY TAKE US FOR?
Wilson, Vincent, and Tommy

WHO I WAS
Tommy and Students

RUNAWAY
Julia

GIMIKWENDEN INA (Do you remember?)
Tommy, Rita, and Students

THIS IS WHAT YOU GET
Full Company

INTERMISSION

AWAY WE RIDE
Wilson, Tommy, Vincent, and Father Christopher

GOD ONLY KNOWS (reprise)
Sister Bernadette, Wilson, and all students

THE CLOSEST THING TO HOME (reprise)
Tommy

HOMEWARD BOUND
Julia

PATER NOSTER (reprise)
Students and Father Christopher

THEIR SPIRITS ARE BROKEN
Sister Bernadette

WONDERLAND
Tommy

AND WE WAIT
Tom and Rita

BAAMAAPII KA WAB MIGO (until we see you again)
Rita, Full Company, and Audience

Setting

Set in two time periods; the first, a residential school in 1950; the second, twenty years later.

A Note About the Text

A forward slash / indicates an overlap in dialogue, i.e. when the next character begins speaking.

An ellipsis … indicates a trail-off of speech.

Text in CAPS is sung.

Text in open brackets ( ) indicates English translation of Ojibway, Cree, and Latin words/phrases.

Act One

Scene 1

> *A drum is heard off in the distance as the sun is coming up on the horizon; standing in the centre of the field is TOM, taking in the sky behind him. From his stance we see that this is the end of a long day; he is slouched, fidgeting, and anxious; tugging at his pant legs as if he's a grown man fighting against his younger self. RITA faces him.*

<u>GOD ONLY KNOWS</u>

RITA: I've only ever seen it from the gate. I was never let past this spot.

> *TOM speaks the words under his breath, voices sing softly off in the distance.*

TOM/ALL: WE'RE FALLING BUT WE WILL NOT TOUCH THE GROUND,

RITA: And now there's a paved road that comes right past the front.

TOM/ALL: THEY SENT US HERE AND THIS IS WHAT WE'VE FOUND,

RITA: I bet most people drive past and have no idea what was here.

TOM/ALL: NOW ALL THEY SAY IS FORCING ITS WAY DOWN,

RITA: No wind blowing, no birds overhead, the air feels stale.

TOM/ALL: WE RUN AWAY, WE'RE RUNNING TO THE SOUND.

RITA: I'm right behind you, Tom.

> *They are interrupted by the loud sound of a train whistle that takes us to 1950. The cast members transform TOM into his younger self as RITA disappears. FATHER CHRISTOPHER is sitting on the back steps of the school; he is smoking when SISTER BERNADETTE enters.*

FATHER: Back to bed, or so help me...

SISTER: It's me, Father.

FATHER: Sister, my apologies. The boys have been testing me the last few nights.

SISTER: No explanation needed. Any suggestions for the removal of odours?

FATHER: What kind of odours?

SISTER: My girls' quarters smell of urine from the other night. There's something about the smell that lingers in the air.

FATHER: If that is your biggest problem, you should be thankful.

> *Boys Dorm – three beds side by side. WILSON is standing on his bed in the centre. The other two boys, TOMMY, now dressed in his school uniform, and VINCENT, are kneeling in front of him.*

WILSON: FIRST THINGS FIRST, WE NEED TO AGREE
THAT WORD OF THIS CAN'T SPREAD BEYOND
US THREE.
IF THIS IS THE PLAN, THEN NO ONE GETS
CAUGHT.
AN HOUR FROM NOW WE'LL TASTE APPLES WE
GOT.

TOMMY: WE ARE HUNGRY,

TOMMY & VINCENT: WE ARE TIRED OF EATING SLOP.

VINCENT: IT'S CHALK AND CRUMBLY,

BOYS: CHOKE IT DOWN BEFORE IT COMES UP.

> *With a flourish, boys start removing their pillows from their pillowcases and preparing for their mission. Boys spin beds and sneak down the hall as girls run to the beds, taking their place. In the Girls' Dorm, JOANNA is standing guard at the door. JULIA is putting on her jacket.*

JOANNA: Sister still hasn't started her bed count.

> *JOANNA hands JULIA apples and bread.*

ELIZABETH: You think they'll fall for that pillow trick again?

JULIA: I'll take my chances. I have to go home.

JOANNA: What about Tommy?

JULIA: I'll come back for him.

> *JULIA starts packing her small bag and adjusting her pillow under her bedsheets to look as if she's asleep. Boys sneak through the field on their mission toward the orchard.*

BOYS: WE'RE FALLING BUT WE WILL NOT TOUCH THE GROUND.

ELIZABETH: HEAR THEM NOW,

JOANNA: HEAR THE SOUND,

BOTH: FOOTSTEPS COMING DOWN THE HALL.

BOYS: THEY SENT US HERE AND THIS IS WHAT WE'VE FOUND.

ELIZABETH: I WAS RIGHT,

JOANNA: NOT TONIGHT,

ELIZABETH: YOU'RE TOO CHICKEN AFTER ALL.

BOYS: NOW ALL THEY SAY IS FORCING ITS WAY DOWN.

JULIA: FORCING ITS WAY DOWN.

JOANNA: We'll cover for you. *(To ELIZABETH.)* Right?

ELIZABETH: Right.

ALL: WE RUN AWAY, WE'RE RUNNING TO THE SOUND.

> *JULIA hugs ELIZABETH and JOANNA, takes her bag and runs off. VINCENT stands on TOMMY's back, picking apples and passing them to WILSON below. Back to the porch.*

FATHER: I have been looking forward to this all day.

SISTER: A cigarette?

FATHER: No, silence. But the cig doesn't hurt.

> *Holds out a cigarette for her.*

SISTER: No, thank you. I should go back in. I haven't done my bed count.

FATHER: Just a drag. Takes the stress off.

> *SISTER leans in and he lights her cigarette.*

SISTER: Happy?

FATHER: Very.

> *SISTER sits and smokes. Back to the boys in the orchard; VINCENT jumps down and they pick up apples that have fallen and put them in their pillowcases.*

WILSON: FATHER WON'T NOTICE, BUT SISTER IS STRICT,
             AND THE MONSIGNOR KNOWS ALL OUR
             TRICKS, SO
             VINCENT STAND GUARD, SO WE DON'T GET
             CAUGHT.
             WE'LL HAVE TO MOVE FAST TO GET THESE
             APPLES BACK UP.

The boys are sneaking back into the school with their apples. They stop at the door, hearing footsteps coming down the hallway towards them. They hide.

TOMMY: SOMEONE'S COMING,

TOMMY & VINCENT:
             SOMEONE'S COMING STRAIGHT DOWN THE HALL.

VINCENT: NOW THEY'RE RUNNING,

BOYS: GET READY TO BOLT OR THEY'LL TAKE US ALL.

They hide as JULIA runs past them in full sprint. She stops at the edge of the field and picks up a red flower. The boys don't see her and sneak back into the school after she passes. They go to their beds.

FATHER CHRISTOPHER & SISTER BERNADETTE:
             GOD ONLY KNOWS WHAT WE'VE BEEN THROUGH.
             IF HE COULD SEE US, WHAT WOULD HE DO?
             GOD ONLY KNOWS HOW MUCH WE TAKE.
             HE ALONE SEES US WHEN WE BREAK.

JULIA: I KNOW THAT I'M FOOLISH TRYING,
             I'LL FOLLOW THE ROAD AHEAD,
             I'M WILLING TO TAKE MY CHANCES INSTEAD.

On the porch again.

FATHER: You know, you are different than the others.

SISTER: What? Why do you say that?

FATHER: You seem good.

SISTER: I am. I am good.

The boys race back to their beds, WILSON gives TOMMY and VINCENT apples and they eat. JOANNA stares out the window as ELIZABETH prays.

FATHER: Then how did you end up here? This isn't where
            the upper crust of the religious institution resides.

            SISTER puts out her cigarette and rushes inside.

ALL CHILDREN: *(Overlapping FATHER & SISTER.)*
                WE'RE FALLING BUT WE WILL NOT TOUCH THE
                GROUND
                THEY SENT US HERE AND THIS IS WHAT WE'VE
                FOUND
                NOW ALL THEY SAY IS FORCING ITS WAY DOWN
                WE RUN AWAY, WE'RE RUNNING TO THE SOUND

                WE'RE RUNNING TO THE SOUND.

FATHER CHRISTOPHER & SISTER BERNADETTE:
                (Overlapping ALL CHILDREN.)
                GOD ONLY KNOWS WHAT WE'VE BEEN
                THROUGH
                IF HE COULD SEE US WHAT WOULD HE DO?
                GOD ONLY KNOWS HOW MUCH WE TAKE
                HE ALONE SEES US WHEN WE BREAK

                WHEN WE BREAK, WE BREAK
                GOD ONLY SEES US WHEN WE BREAK
                WHEN WE BREAK, WE BREAK
                WHEN WE BREAK.

                Transition into Act One Scene 2 (music).

Scene 2

> *RITA is folding laundry. She has long grey hair and is wearing baggy clothes. TOM is in the other room.*

TOM: (*Offstage.*) Hey Ma, have you seen my jacket?

RITA: Your what?

TOM: (*Offstage.*) My jacket.

RITA: Which one? The brown or black?

TOM: (*Offstage.*) Brown.

> *TOM enters, buttoning up his dress shirt collar.*

RITA: This one?

> *Points to the jacket on the couch.*

TOM: Ya. I've been lookin' in there for five minutes, you coulda told me it was out here.

> *Phone rings.*

RITA: I can't read your damn mind. Your shirt is untucked at the back.

> *TOM answers.*

TOM: Yeah. Hey, Bucko...no, I don't have time... (*Pause.*) Slow down. Will you shut up? Hey, put your Ma on? Just for a second. Listen to your father, put her on. (*Pause.*) I'll beat your ass when I get home if you keep this up. I can hear her in the background – you little shit.

> *RITA waves frantically but TOM ignores her.*

Ya, ya. Grandma says "Hi."

> *He waves back at her.*

No she's busy, Buck. Listen, I gotta go, you're gonna make me late.

> *Hangs up phone.*

RITA:	Are you blind? I was waving like a damn fool over here. I would like to talk to my grandkids. You should have brought them with you. It would have been nice to have them running around the house making a mess of the place.
TOM:	Ma, this place is already a mess.
RITA:	But with the kids around, at least we would have an excuse. (*Laughs.*)
TOM:	Sandy doesn't like them comin' up here.
RITA:	Hey, bring Sandy too! I'll put up with that Sasquatch to spend a few days with my boys. I won't start nothin', honest.
TOM:	No.
RITA:	Don't be stubborn. When was the last time you talked to her?
TOM:	Were you not just standing here? I tried to talk to her.
RITA:	Why don't I call? I've got the magic touch. They could make it here in a few hours…
TOM:	Hey, you oughta mind your own business.
RITA:	Sorry. Sorry for wanting to see my own grandsons.
TOM:	Yeah well…so do I.
RITA:	I was even willing to put up with that mess of a mother. Do you know what a big step that is for me?
TOM:	Ma, last time she was here you told her if she came back on reserve she would get shot.
RITA:	Good advice.
TOM:	That hunters would mistake her for a moose.
RITA:	She's got long legs, Tom.

TOM:	See! And you wonder why she won't come up here. She'll talk to me when I get this job today.
RITA:	Which one is it this time?
TOM:	The shipping one. I have a good feeling about it.
RITA:	Like the feeling you had with the last one?
TOM:	What do you know about working a job?
RITA:	I help out at the band office.
TOM:	You think answering the phone counts? Gossiping with the Aunties is a full-time job now.
RITA:	Me and the Aunties will kick your ass if you keep this up.
TOM:	I need to take off.

TOM turns to face RITA who is surprised by how he looks.

YOUR FATHER

TOM:	What? Why are you looking at me funny?
RITA:	It's nothing. (Pause.) Wait. I have something for you.

She runs offstage.

TOM:	Ma, you're gonna make me late.

She returns with a small red pouch with tobacco in it.

RITA:	YOU LOOK JUST LIKE YOUR FATHER YOU LOOK JUST LIKE HIM BEFORE HE WENT AWAY I KNOW THAT HE COULDN'T BE PROUDER HE'D WANT YOU TO HAVE THIS TODAY

Here.

TOM:	No.

RITA: It was your father's…

TOM: Ma, why don't you stamp my status number on my forehead while you're at it?

RITA: Oh, ha ha ha!

TOM: I don't wanna look like an Indian today.

RITA: Good luck with that. I get it. Go, go! You'll be late.

> *TOM takes the pouch from her hands. RITA holds his hand. TOM tries to pull away, but RITA pulls him back without breaking focus. Her eyes are closed.*

TOM: I'll see you later.

RITA: Give him strength, protect him in his travels, oh Lord. We are your sons and daughters, have us do your work. In your name we pray. Amen.

> *She opens her eyes and crosses herself; TOM does not.*

Good luck, Son.

> *TOM leaves.*

YOU WILL LEAVE LIKE YOUR FATHER DID
YOU WILL LEAVE ME ALL ALONE
FOR A SHORT TIME, IT MIGHT SEEM ALL RIGHT
BUT YEARS DISAPPEAR OVERNIGHT.

YOU LOOK JUST LIKE YOUR FATHER
YOU LOOK JUST LIKE HIM BEFORE HE WENT
AWAY.

Scene 3

> *Back to 1950. The next morning, FATHER CHRISTOPHER escorts JULIA up the school driveway, meeting SISTER BERNADETTE standing on the front steps.*

SISTER: Julia, give me your bag and get inside.

JULIA: Yes, Sister.

> *She drops her bag and walks towards SISTER BERNADETTE. JULIA runs offstage quickly.*

SISTER: I'm sorry, Father Christopher. Where did you find her?

FATHER: I did not. The police found her on the highway walking toward town. They brought her to the front gate and I met them there.

SISTER: I don't know how I missed her in the bed count. I...I will keep an eye on her.

FATHER: Have you had a chance to walk through the orchard since you have been here?

SISTER: No, I haven't had much free time. Oh and I used vinegar on the sheets, and the smell is gone.

FATHER: Monsignor used to spend all his time pruning and trimming these trees. It relaxed him. The day-to-day efforts producing a sweet and delicious fruit in the fall.

SISTER: Perhaps I should take up pruning.

FATHER: It takes discipline and constant attention. And from what I see, your approach with your girls is not one to be admired.

SISTER: I did everything I was told to do.

FATHER: Then how did Julia end up a mile from our grounds? Did you even bother to do your bed check?

SISTER: I did my count. She was in bed when I checked.
             I know it.

FATHER: Sister Bernadette, discipline needs to be enforced
             and its lack will ferment this kind of behaviour.

SISTER: I know, Father. She's only running for attention.
             I will have a talk with her.

FATHER: Much more than talk is needed for this type of
             behaviour. Whenever one of my boys has run, he
             is stripped, hosed, and left in the dark cellar to
             think about his actions.

SISTER: I want to get through to her without resorting to
             isolation.

FATHER: Until she makes it past town next time? How far
             does she have to get for you to understand that
             your methods are not effective?

SISTER: I understand. I am sorry for questioning you.
             I will do what needs to be done...

             FATHER CHRISTOPHER starts to exit.

             Father Christopher, forgive me. This will not
             happen again, I assure you. I pray that tonight's
             event will not reach Monsignor. As it was only a
             one-time occurrence, I beg you.

FATHER: Sister, this is not the first time and it will not be
             the last. Monsignor may know but rest assured,
             it will not come from me.

SISTER: Thank you for your silence.

PATER NOSTER

             *FATHER enters the school; SISTER
             BERNADETTE picks up Julia's bag and
             follows him.*

Scene 4

Students enter the chapel in an orderly fashion. They kneel. FATHER CHRISTOPHER and SISTER BERNADETTE stand behind them as they all sing.

ALL: Mm…
PATER NOSTER (Our Father),
QUI ES IN CEALIS (Who art in heaven)
SANCTIFICETUR NOMEN TUUM (Hallowed be Thy name)

PATER NOSTER (Our Father),
QUI ES IN CEALIS (Who art in heaven),
AMEN.

The students stand and leave the chapel while humming. TOMMY breaks off and hides, crouched behind a line of shrubs where he waits. JULIA crawls in between the trees and rushes to him.

TOMMY: *Ondaas, Nimise* (Come here, Sister), there you are!

They jump into each other's arms.

You're late. We said we would meet at our secret hiding spot when the shadow of this rock meets this twig.

JULIA: Tommy. I can explain.

TOMMY: The shadow is past the *wadikwan* (twig), Julia.

JULIA: I know.

TOMMY: When we heard someone had run, the guys were sure it was you. But I told 'em "That's my sister, and she's not going anywhere without me!" And I was right. Just wait till I tell Wilson, he'll eat his words!

JULIA: Tommy, listen…

TOMMY: So who was it, huh? No, don't tell me, I want to guess…that little girl with the short black hair.

JULIA: We all have short hair.

TOMMY: I was kidding. That one doesn't count. Was it…

JULIA: It was a girl in fourth year. Got scared and bolted, I guess.

TOMMY: Wow, a brave move for a fourth-year. It's not even that bad yet.

JULIA: She was a bed-wetter, couldn't make it through the night.

TOMMY: She get the pee parade?

JULIA: Yeah, all the time.

TOMMY: Vince was the worst bed-wetter, but me and Wilson would change his sheets before Father would wake up so he wouldn't get the pee parade. You should do that.

JULIA: You guys look after your own. I like that. Were you here when the train passed?

TOMMY: Yeah, I was. But *Nimaamaa* (Mom) didn't come.

JULIA: Are you surprised?

TOMMY: I've been writing to her, you know. Told her to come get us. So she's gonna come any day now.

JULIA: You think they sent your letter?

TOMMY: Yah. Why wouldn't they send it?

JULIA: If your letter says anything about wanting to go home, they won't send it. I thought you knew that.

TOMMY: No, I didn't know.

JULIA: Your hair is so short – you look different than I
          remember.

TOMMY: *Gimikwenden ina.* (Tell me what you remember.)

JULIA: What I remember? Tommy, your hair used to be
          longer, don't be dumb.

TOMMY: I mean about home. I remember the smallest
          things so clearly but some things are blurring
          together…

JULIA: Tommy, you gotta get out of here. If they see us
          talking we'll get a good lickin' for sure.

THE CLOSEST THING TO HOME

BOTH: *Stl'ek!* (Nun!)

          *They both duck behind the shrubs. SISTER
          BERNADETTE and FATHER CHRISTOPHER
          come rushing and pass them without notice.
          SISTER BERNADETTE is carrying Julia's bag.*

TOMMY: I'VE BEEN TRYING TO WRITE IT ALL
          FROM WHAT I CAN REMEMBER
          I'M EVEN WILLING TO TAKE THE FALL
          IF FATHER FINDS ME OUT

          I KNOW IT'S DIFFICULT LOOKING BACK
          ON YEARS BEFORE WE CAME HERE
          BUT THOSE YEARS ARE ALL I HAVE
          AND I NEED TO MAKE THEM CLEAR

          I REMEMBER THE GRAVEL ROADS
          AND DUST WOULD GET ALL OVER
          MA WOULD YELL AT US TO GET CLEAN
          WHEN WE CAME IN FROM THE FIELD

          I CAN SOMETIMES HEAR THE DRUMS
          IF I CLOSE MY EYES AND DREAM IT
          THEIR BEATING IS CALLING ME
          AND WILL GUIDE ME SAFELY HOME.

THEY SAY WE SHOULD FORGET IT ALL
THEY SAY IT ALL MAKES US BAD
THESE MEMORIES I WON'T OUTGROW
AND YOU'RE THE CLOSEST THING TO HOME
I KNOW.

I SEE THE TRAILS IN OUR BACKYARD
AND THE FORT WE BUILT WITH PAPA
I REMEMBER WE'D EAT MOOSE STEW
UNTIL WE WERE SO FULL

I CAN HEAR US LAUGHING LOUD
SO MUCH MY TUMMY ACHING
I DON'T THINK I HAVE HEARD YOU LAUGH
AT ALL SINCE WE'VE BEEN HERE

I WANNA HEAR ALL THE SIGHTS AND SOUNDS
EVEN THOUGH YOU THINK IT'S POINTLESS
I REMIND MYSELF EVERY DAY
UNTIL I MAKE IT STICK

JULIA: STOP BEING STUBBORN AND LOOK AROUND
           JUST LOOK AND SEE IT'S HOPELESS
           KEEP QUIET AND YOUR HEAD DOWN,
           AND YOU'LL BLEND IN LIKE THE REST

BOTH: THEY SAY WE SHOULD FORGET IT ALL
           THEY SAY IT ALL MAKES US BAD
           THESE MEMORIES WE WON'T OUTGROW
           AND YOU'RE THE CLOSEST THING TO HOME
           I KNOW.

TOMMY: You don't remember anything?

JULIA: It has been ten years, Tommy. I'm not sure if what
           I remember really happened or if I made it up to
           make myself feel better.

TOMMY: I don't care, just tell me.

JULIA: No, Tommy. Quit it.

TOMMY: *Daga.* (Please.)

JULIA: Piss off, no.

TOMMY: You remember…

JULIA: Don't do that to yourself, Tommy.

TOMMY: *Nimise* (Sister), I need to know.

JULIA: I REMEMBER ALL OF IT STILL
           I CAN SEE YOU RUNNING UP OUR HILL
           I CAN HEAR THOSE DRUMS BEAT.
           I CAN FEEL THE GROUND
           TOUCH MY BARE FEET.

BOTH: THE CLOSEST THING TO LIFE,
           THE CLOSEST THING TO HOME,
           YOU'RE THE CLOSEST THING TO LOVE I KNOW.

TOMMY: We should run together.

JULIA: We will. Get out of here! If they beat me to my
           bed, I'll get it.

TOMMY: *Bekaa!* (Wait!) If you get word from home, promise
           you'll tell me.

JULIA: I promise. Now go!

           *She starts pushing him. They hug and sneak off
           in opposite directions.*

Scene 5

> *A telephone rings, and a SECRETARY behind a reception desk answers it. She takes a message. TOM rushes into the waiting room and walks over to her desk.*

TOM: Are they still here? Sorry, I had an interview this morning but…when did they change the speed limit in town? Fifty the whole way? That's new, huh?

SECRETARY: It's been that way for a while. You don't live here?

TOM: No, I don't. I would if I got hired, you know. I did before. I shouldn't ask this but…how many others have been interviewed for this job? Sorry that's…ugh, none of my business. (*Pause.*) Ballpark figures? How many? Give or take.

SECRETARY: You're right. That's none of your business.

TOM: Sorry. I'm…very sorry.

> *She walks to the office door.*

SECRETARY: Mr. Sekora, we're waiting on your two o'clock, but one of the "no-shows" from this morning has arrived if you'd like to see him now…

WILSON: (*Offstage.*) Give me a minute.

SECRETARY: You heard him. He'll be a minute.

TOM: Did you say Sekora?

SECRETARY: Yes.

TOM: What? It's Wilson Sekora, right?

SECRETARY: Yes.

TOM: I know him. We know each other, right. What are the chances?

SECRETARY: I'm guessing, pretty good.

TOM: … We…we go way back… He's got his own office
                  and all. Son of a bitch has done good for himself,
                  hasn't he? Couches and everything! I mean, that's
                  a good-looking couch. When I knew Wilson he
                  was a shit-disturber – couldn't stay out of trouble.
                  He still like that? Still making trouble?

SECRETARY: No, not at all.

                  *WILSON enters and hands a stack of letters to
                  his SECRETARY.*

WILSON: Send these out today, if you can manage.

TOM: Wilson Sekora.

WILSON: Tommy. No way… I thought your name sounded
                  familiar on my list. Come on in. This is wild, eh?

                  They shake hands. TOM doesn't move.

TOM: … Isn't it? (*Pause.*) Yeah, I mean. Wild!

WILSON: Well, come in. (*Pause.*) Tommy, get in here!

                  TOM snaps out of it.

TOM: Right, yeah. (*Aside.*) No one calls me Tommy
                  anymore.

                  *TOM enters WILSON's office. Beautiful furniture
                  with large paintings; the one behind his desk is a
                  large red painting.*

                  Wow, man. This is your office?

WILSON: Naw. This is just the sitting area, my office is
                  much larger and behind that door.

TOM: Really?

WILSON: No, Jesus, Tommy, I'm playing with you; still a
                  little slow after all these years. Can I make you
                  a drink?

TOM: No. Thanks.

> *WILSON takes a bottle of whiskey out of his desk and pours two glasses.*

WILSON: If I had known it was you I wouldn't have made you wait.

TOM: It's no problem. I was chatting up your secretary. I think she's got her eye on me. Playin' hard to get.

WILSON: Oh yeah?

TOM: She pick out all these big paintings for you?

> *WILSON hands a drink to TOM, who puts it back down on the desk.*

WILSON: I asked the guys upstairs what do the other managers have on their walls. This is what they sent. Some Indian artist.

TOM: That's what I thought. Looks Indian.

WILSON: Cheers.

> *WILSON drinks. TOM does not.*

You have a wife and kids?

TOM: Two boys.

WILSON: Oh yeah?

TOM: You? Kids, wife, all of it?

> *TOM puts his drink down on the table.*

WILSON: Yeah. Two of each.

TOM: Wives or kids? Ah?

WILSON: Four kids. And the wife, well she's different than you would expect me to marry, I'm sure. But she's a good one, her father was a police officer so she was raised right.

TOM: Good.

WILSON: It's been a long time, eh? Look at us now.

TOM toasts and WILSON drinks.

TOM: Funny how things work out.

WILSON: Do you fix houses? My wife wanted this place on the lake, but it's old and doesn't have a good foundation. Roof is caving in. We got it against my better judgement but now we have to just throw money at it. I'm looking for someone to fix it up. We got to make the wives happy, am I right?

TOM: Ya. Well, my wife will be happy if I get a job on the front lines here.

WILSON: Right, your application. I forgot you were even here for…

TOM: I'm real good with people and in high-stress situations. I'm a fast learner and am always on time. I figure that's important, right?

WILSON: You were late today!

TOM: Yeah. Right, but…

WILSON: I, uh, see you have here that you finished school? Did you go back and finish?

TOM: Well, I just put that there to show that…

WILSON: Went somewhere else to finish it, did ya?

TOM: You know, that's funny, cause I've wanted to for years, eh! I've even thought of…

WILSON: Come on, Tommy. You can't bullshit me. I know you didn't finish.

TOM: I didn't but I still think I'd be a great fit here.

WILSON: Tommy, it's a shame. I really wish I could help. But I can't swing it that way.

TOM: No, no, wait – I'd work harder than anyone, you know that.

WILSON: My boss. He'd never approve it. He's the hardass here. Wouldn't let me sneak one by who never made it past Grade 8. We'll keep you on our list for future hires. And we'll see what comes up in a few weeks.

TOM: I don't have a few weeks.

WILSON: It's the best I can do, Tommy.

TOM: Don't call me Tommy! No one has called me that since – sorry, thanks anyway for your time.

TOM begins to leave.

WILSON: Listen, I'm done here in a couple of hours, wanna go for a drink?

TOM: I can't.

WILSON: Come on. It's on me. It's the least I can do. There's a place two blocks north on Whitewood, it's a dive but no one will be there on a weeknight. How about there, around six?

TOM: OK.

WILSON: For old times.

TOM: Yeah.

TOM exits.

Transition into Act One Scene 6 (music).

Scene 6

> *WILSON and VINCENT are writing at their desks and FATHER CHRISTOPHER is making notes on the chalkboard. JOANNA and ELIZABETH are in the Girls' Dorm scrubbing the floors on their hands and knees. JOANNA is distracted.*

JOANNA: I can't believe she almost made it to town.

ELIZABETH: Almost.

JOANNA: Most kids I hear just get a ways down the road or 'round by the field before being dragged back. I'd like to see how far you would get.

ELIZABETH: Julia can run all she wants but that doesn't mean I have to.

JOANNA: And what is this, the third time? Guess she's going after Big John's record.

ELIZABETH: Maybe if she did her work, ol' Bernie would cut her some slack.

JOANNA: It's not the same when you're taken like they were. Your parents bring you to town every Sunday. They haven't even been home once. *(Proudly.)* I'll run when I'm older.

ELIZABETH: Big talk.

JOANNA: I'm serious, I even know where I'd go, straight up over Cow Mountain. They wouldn't follow me there.

ELIZABETH: You think she ran because of her "friend"?

JOANNA: What? Whose friend?

ELIZABETH: Oh you know, her moon time.

JOANNA: Why would that matter?

ELIZABETH: She's older than us.

JOANNA: Maybe she got it and couldn't stop the bleeding so she ran to the hospital.

> *ELIZABETH splashes JOANNA with the scrub brush from her bucket and they laugh. In the Boys' Classroom TOMMY enters.*

FATHER: Tommy, come in. Where have you been all evening? Getting a head start on tomorrow's readings?

TOMMY: Donno.

FATHER: Language, Tommy. Speak properly.

TOMMY: Sorry, Father. I do not know where I was. I must have lost track of time.

FATHER: Much better. You almost missed all the fun. We are having a good time, aren't we, boys?

WILSON & VINCENT: Yes, sir.

FATHER: Take out a piece of paper and a pencil, then we will begin.

WILSON: (*Whispering.*) Tommy, out in the field again?

TOMMY: (*Whispering.*) What's it to you?

FATHER: No talking.

> *WILSON takes VINCENT's pencil.*

VINCENT: Father, Wilson stole my p...encil.

WILSON: It's not stealing when you're related. Besides, he needs to learn how to share.

FATHER: Wilson, give the pencil back. You can use mine.

WILSON goes to front of the class, gets a pencil and when he returns he mimics FATHER CHRISTOPHER. They laugh.

You will copy down this letter exactly and we can send them home for your parents to see how you are doing.

FATHER turns and starts writing the letter home on the chalkboard and reads as he writes.

"Dear Mother and Father,

How are you? I am well. (*Overlapping.*) I have been learning how to read and write. I am behaving most of the time and am rewarded with fresh-grown apples from the orchard when I do my chores."

WILSON: (*Overlapping, whispering.*) Where were you?

TOMMY: (*Whispering.*) At our secret spot.

VINCENT: (*Whispering.*) Shush up, you'll get us in t...t... trouble.

WILSON: (*Whispering, mockingly.*) Shush up, you'll get us in t...t...trouble.

WILSON pushes VINCENT's face back with his hand.

TOMMY: Did you know that they don't even send our letters home? Julia said they read them, and if you say anything bad they rip them up.

VINCENT: What? Really? But I got a letter back a few months ago.

WILSON: You didn't bad-mouth the school in it, did ya?

VINCENT: No. I just copied what Father put on the board.

TOMMY: See. That's what they want. No wonder my Ma hasn't come to get us. I know if she got my letters, and heard how bad it was here, she would.

SISTER BERNADETTE enters.

SISTER: Father, a moment please.

FATHER: *(To students.)* Keep writing. *(To SISTER.)* What is it?

SISTER: Another letter from Indian Affairs. How did you reply in the past?

FATHER: Tell them that the money was used on improvements for the school and we are still working out how much needs to be done to this old wreck. We need to post a surplus.

SISTER: I will need you to look it over.

FATHER: All right, let's do it now.

> *FATHER CHRISTOPHER and SISTER BERNADETTE leave down the hall.*

WHAT DO THEY TAKE US FOR?

WILSON: THEY THINK YOU DON'T HAVE A BRAIN
A SAVAGE THEY CAN TAME
TO FOLLOW THEIR OWN MOTTO.

VINCENT: THEY THINK WE LIVE IN DIRT
WITH FEELINGS THEY CAN'T HURT
AND RULES WE HAVE TO FOLLOW.

BOTH: THEY'RE PLAYING GAMES WITH OUR HEADS
FROM CHAPEL 'TIL WE HIT OUR BEDS
WE WRITE LETTERS THEY DON'T SEND
WE WAKE UP PRAYING THIS WILL END.

WILSON: WHAT DO THEY TAKE US FOR?

> *WILSON runs to the front of the class.*

TOMMY: What are we supposed to do?

WILSON: We're on to them.

VINCENT: Yeah. We should write home so our Ma and Pa
                can read it.

WILSON: Right. Vince, watch for Father at the door.

TOMMY: How do we do that?

WILSON: You have to change the letter.

TOMMY: Me? Why me?

WILSON: YOU'VE GOT A WAY WITH WORDS
                YOU KNOW YOUR NOUNS AND VERBS
                AND WRITE JUST LIKE THE FATHER.

                DON'T BE A SCAREDY CAT
                I PROMISE NOT TO RAT
                YOU OUT TO ANY OTHER.

WILSON & VINCENT:
                WE'RE COUNTING ON YOU THIS TIME
                DON'T LOOK AT US LIKE IT'S A CRIME
                WRITE DOWN WORDS THAT WE CHOOSE
                AND FOR ONCE BREAK THE RULES.

WILSON: WHAT DO THEY TAKE US FOR?

VINCENT: WHAT DO THEY TAKE US FOR?

BOTH: WHAT DO THEY TAKE US FOR?

TOMMY: I can't. I can't remember.

WILSON: OK, then write it in English. Maybe...

                *TOMMY and WILSON go to the front of the class
                and begin erasing and replacing words on the
                chalkboard. They giggle. VINCENT is looking
                out the window.*

VINCENT: CLOSE YOUR EYES AND REMEMBER
            ALL THAT WAS BEFORE
            AUTUMN CHILLY SEPTEMBER
            WHO COULD HAVE KNOWN
            WHAT WE WOULD HAVE IN STORE.

            VINCENT rushes to the classroom door.

WILSON: WHAT DO THEY TAKE US FOR?

TOMMY: WHAT DO THEY TAKE US FOR?

VINCENT: He's coming back!

ALL: WHAT DO THEY TAKE US FOR?
            WHAT DO THEY TAKE US FOR?
            WHAT DO THEY TAKE US FOR?

            *The boys flip the chalkboard over, run around
            the room, and return to their desks. They sit as
            the song ends and put their heads down as if
            they were writing just as FATHER appears at
            the door.*

FATHER: Are you done with your letters?

            *The boys don't answer. He walks over to
            the chalkboard and flips it over. The letter is
            revealed and the boys laugh.*

            "Dear MA and PA,

            How are you? I am INDIAN. I have been learning
            how to BE A WHITE MAN. I am behaving ALL
            THE TIME and am rewarded by fresh grown SLOP
            from the PREIST when I do my chores..."

            Who is responsible for this?

WILSON: Why are you lookin' at me? I'm not the only one
            in here.

FATHER: Well, if you didn't do it then you orchestrated this
            vulgarity.

FATHER CHRISTOPHER slaps WILSON, grabs him by the ear, pulls him to the front of the class, and throws him violently to the ground. The other boys put their heads down. WILSON is crouched at the front of the class awaiting punishment.

FATHER: This behaviour shows us you will never change. A weak mind, with no intelligence – like the dirty savages that have come before you. I am not surprised by this. Now…what is the punishment for ignorant boys? Vincent?

VINCENT: They get a slap?

FATHER: For this disgusting offence? We need something that will get through to this stubborn mule. Tommy?

TOMMY: No meals for…a week?

FATHER: I think that is appropriate. Thank you, very good, Tommy. I will also expect fifty lines of "I will not disrupt the class" by the end of the day. Now erase this filth. The rest of you, finish your letters.

JOANNA and ELIZABETH in the Girls' Dorm again. JULIA enters.

JOANNA: Julia! Did you get the strap?

JULIA: Not yet. But I think I know what's comin'. I won't eat for a week, I'm sure.

ELIZABETH: You shouldn't have run. I told you it wouldn't work. And now we're going to be strapped for helping you.

JULIA: What's this?

Points to the book in her hand.

ELIZABETH: Nothing. My parents gave it to me last week when they took me to town for lunch.

JULIA: Is it any good? If I read one more Bible passage I will rip my eyes out.

ELIZABETH: I don't know. I've only just started it.

JOANNA: It's about a white girl named Alice.

ELIZABETH: She can find out on her own...some people can read, you know.

JOANNA: I can read. Just not so good. And besides, I like when people read to me, making all the silly voices.

JULIA: I'll read you every word. I found these red *waabigwaniin* (flowers) just off the path to the main road.

                 She puts her hand in her pocket and pulls out a handful of red flowers.

JOANNA: Oh, can you put one in my hair?

JULIA: Here.

                 JOANNA turns around and JULIA puts the flower in her hair.

ELIZABETH: They look like weeds to me. We don't have them in our field because the barn animals eat everything before it has a chance to bloom.

JULIA: Well, I've never seen one like this before. I want to go back and pick some more. You can come with me, I remember where they are.

JOANNA: How many are there?

JULIA: Just past the forest there's a field full of them, all in bloom. I don't know how they survive this long hidden away all alone.

                 They hear footsteps coming down the hallway.

ELIZABETH: Are you crazy? Hide them.

SISTER BERNADETTE enters and the girls remove the flowers from their hair and stuff them in their pockets.

SISTER: I don't even know where to begin with you girls. What do I have to do to get through to you? From today, things will change. All of you will be punished for anyone who acts out of line. Maybe then you will think twice before supporting one of your foolish classmates. Julia, come here, please. Hold out your hands.

JOANNA: (*Whispering.*) Don't make a sound.

JULIA walks over to SISTER and kneels in front of her. JOANNA and ELIZABETH turn away and flinch with each whip.

SISTER: (*Whip.*) You no longer have privilege to the grounds. (*Whip.*) You will not be privileged to meals until you can appreciate what we provide for you; (*Whip.*) you will be expected to pray on your knees until they are bruised and aching; if you cannot follow these instructions you will no longer have me to face but the Monsignor as well who will have no mercy in your punishments.

JULIA nods.

Good. Follow me.

JULIA: Yes, Sister.

SISTER leaves the dorm with JULIA following behind, JOANNA gives a tiny wave. FATHER CHRISTOPHER claps twice.

FATHER: All right, boys! Time for bed.

All boys get up to leave. FATHER reaches out and grabs TOMMY's shoulder.

Tommy, stay, please.

VINCENT: What? Why?

WILSON: That's not fair.

FATHER: Life isn't fair; now both of you to bed.

>   *WILSON walks up to TOMMY and shoves him.*

WILSON: You think you're smart, don't you?

>   *FATHER grabs WILSON by the neck and tosses him toward the door.*

FATHER: Save that kind of energy for tomorrow. We'll get out the boxing gloves and you two can duke it out in the gym. But not in here, Sekora.

>   *WILSON turns and exits, VINCENT follows him.*

TOMMY: I can take care of myself.

FATHER: Tommy, I know you were in the field after dark again tonight. I don't know what I have to do to get through to you.

TOMMY: How did you know?

FATHER: I know all and see all, don't forget that. I just want to make sure that you are careful and that you don't freeze out there in that field. It's so cold out there, you could freeze your nose off. If this happens again, I will be forced to make you go without meals.

TOMMY: I understand, Father.

FATHER: Good. Now, tell the others you were punished so they won't be jealous.

>   *FATHER exits into the hallway, leaning on the wall, watching the girls scrubbing the floors off in the distance. TOMMY grabs his paper and pencil and begins writing furiously.*

<u>WHO I WAS</u>

TOMMY: FOR THE FIRST TIME IT'S NOT AN IMAGE
FOR THE FIRST TIME IT'S NOT A SOUND
FOR THE FIRST TIME IT'S A REAL MEMORY
QUICK BEFORE IT'S GONE, WRITE IT DOWN

THIS IS THE START OF WHAT I REMEMBER
THIS IS THE START OF WHAT I LOST
THIS IS THE START OF WHAT MA TOLD US
MAYBE THIS IS WHO I WAS

So they won't send my letter in English, then I'll write it in MY language…to the Chief and send it in town myself. Then the whole village will know it's time to come get us. We're ready to go home now.

ALL STUDENTS:
THEY JUST DON'T KNOW
THEY WOULD KNOW IF THEY CAME HERE
THAT WE'VE HAD ENOUGH
ENOUGH

TOMMY begins writing again.

Aaniin (I see your light)… How do you spell Chief? Why would they not teach us a word we use so much? If I were teaching, that would be the first word I would teach. Chief Chief Indian Chief! Chief Chief Indian Chief! Chief Chief INDIAN CHIEF!!! CHIEF CHIEF INDIAN CHIEF!!!

TOMMY marches around as if he were a Chief and crouches to begin writing again. FATHER CHRISTOPHER approaches ELIZABETH and JOANNA scrubbing floors.

FATHER: Girls, shouldn't you be in your dorm preparing for bed? Your prayers should not be put off. Scrub those hands. Get the brown out.

ELIZABETH: Yes, Father.

FATHER: Joanna, where is…? Was Julia the runner?

JOANNA: She was taken down to the cellar. Sister took her.

FATHER: She was slipping back into her old ways. Quite a harsh punishment.

ELIZABETH: Yes.

FATHER: Would you like it if I checked on her? Brought her food and blankets for you?

JOANNA: That would be very nice.

FATHER: Good. Now go on to bed.

> *JOANNA and ELIZABETH grab the bucket and scrub brushes and exit; FATHER CHRISTOPHER watches them go, then exits.*

TOMMY: I BET JULIA WILL REMEMBER
             IT'S ON THE TIP OF HER TONGUE
             SHE WILL FINISH OFF MY LETTER
             WE'LL SEND IT OFF WITH THE SUN

ALL CAST (*Except TOMMY*):
             GIMIKWENDEN INA (Do you remember)

ALL CAST (*Including TOMMY*):
             THEY JUST DON'T KNOW
             THEY WOULD KNOW IF THEY CAME HERE
             THAT WE'VE HAD ENOUGH
             ENOUGH

TOMMY: WORD WILL MAKE IT HOME AND THEN THE CHIEF WILL READ IT
             WORD WILL MAKE IT HOME BACK TO MY MA
             THEY WILL MAKE IT HERE BEFORE THE WEEK IS OVER
             THEY WILL TAKE US HOME TO WHO I WAS
             WHO I WAS

> *He transforms into TOM waiting in the bar.*

Scene 7

In the bar, TOM is waiting with a drink in his hands as WILSON enters.

TOM: WHO I WAS

            Music ends.

WILSON: Hi, sorry I'm late. I didn't mean to keep you…
            I hope there are no hard feelings about today.
            It's not personal, you know that…right? (*Pause.*)
            It's just business, yeah? I've got a plan for
            you, Tommy. Sorry, I mean Tom. What are you
            drinking? Next one's on me.

TOM: I know. It's just business.

WILSON: Nothing personal. You know, I put you to the top
            of the file, and I have some ideas for how…

TOM: You and your ideas. You were such a shit-
            disturber in school. You remember that? You and
            Vincent. God…you two ran that school.

WILSON: We all grow up, don't we?

TOM: How is your brother doing? I hope he finished
            school; old Vinnie seemed like he could hack it. I
            bet he would have got the job today. Hard worker,
            good with people…

WILSON: … How about your family?

TOM: MY family, oh GOD – (*Sarcastically imitating
            WILSON from earlier.*) my wife, well she's different
            than you would expect me to marry. She's four
            hundred pounds and her toenails can chop wood.
            But her father's a police officer and he raised
            her right.

WILSON: Jesus, Tommy. I think we got off on the wrong
            foot here.

TOM: Yeah, all you've got is the wrong foot.

WILSON: I didn't mean anything by it.

TOM: You tell me to come to a dive bar so your work friends don't see you talking to an Indian. This act has done good for you, huh? Pretending to be a white man, forgetting where you came from. You're the whitewashing they wanted us to be.

WILSON: You don't know what you're talking about.

TOM: What is this? You wanted to catch up. So let's catch up! Go! What do you wanna know?

WILSON: We all went through that shit and at some point you have to suck it up and get over it, man. Now, I've got a few ideas for you…

> *TOM, in one gulp, downs his drink and slams his glass on the table.*

TOM: I need a drink.

WILSON: I'll get it.

TOM: I don't need your charity. If I want a drink, I'll buy it.

> *TOM exits.*

WILSON: Okay. I didn't mean…

> *Transition into Act One Scene 8 (music).*

Scene 8

JULIA is sitting on the floor of a dark cellar. A tray of food slides under the door.

JULIA: Hello, please! I know you can hear me. *Daga, beindigain!* (Please, come in!)

SISTER opens the door as the hall lights blind JULIA.

SISTER: What did you say?

JULIA: I'm sorry, I thought you were Tommy.

SISTER: Never let me hear you speak your devil tongue again or you'll be lucky to get the cellar.

JULIA: Confession! I have a confession, please, I want forgiveness.

SISTER: Save your confession for the Father.

JULIA: What if I'm what they warn about at chapel? I'm a sinner and I want to stop.

SISTER: We are all sinners. You made the choice to run, have you asked God to forgive you for that?

JULIA: Anywhere but here.

SISTER: I know what you're trying to do.

JULIA: He'll come tonight, Sister.

SISTER: I will not entertain this kind of talk from a student. Haven't you caused enough trouble this week? I think so.

JULIA: He comes when I'm alone. I'm afraid, please, you have to believe me…

SISTER: If one of the boys is bothering you, swat him away. Who is it? Julia, tell me that then.

JULIA: I can't say.

SISTER: Liar! Making up these kind of stories is the work of the devil. I will not listen to another word…

> *SISTER begins to leave the cellar.*

JULIA: …I wouldn't make it up, honest. He comes when I'm alone…

SISTER: Shut up! (*Pause.*) Now, I demand that you ask forgiveness for your sins.

RUNAWAY

JULIA: ASK FOR FORGIVENESS? I TELL THE TRUTH

SISTER: You will never speak of this again.

JULIA: PRAY FOR FORGIVENESS, FOR ALL MY YOUTH

SISTER: And I will add an extra ten lashings for being a liar.

JULIA: GOD-LOVING MAN SAYS HE'S LOVING ME

SISTER: Now get down on your knees,

JULIA: AND I HOPE FOR THE DAY

SISTER: and hold out your hands.

JULIA: THAT YOU WILL SEE.

> *JULIA kneels down and gives her hands to SISTER. She cringes but does not make a sound as the whipping starts. She stands and witnesses herself being whipped.*

WHO IS SHE, THIS GIRL STARES BACK AT ME
WHO IS SHE, I WISH THAT I COULD SEE
IS IT HER, THE GIRL WHO HAD MY MOTHER'S EYES
IS IT HER, THE GIRL WHO'S BEATEN DOWN INSIDE.

TAKE AWAY THE WALLS SURROUNDING ME
MANY RUN AWAY AFRAID OF WHAT THEY'LL BE
CAN'T YOU COME IN CLOSE AND HOLD ME
TIGHT, LORD
CAN'T YOU HEAR ME CRYING IN THE NIGHT,
LORD
TAKE AWAY THIS PAIN INSIDE OF ME
RUN AWAY, WE'RE RUNNING TO BE FREE.

> *The whipping ends. After a moment, SISTER turns, exits, and locks the door.*

FOR YEARS I'VE BEEN HIS LITTLE GIRL, HIS
SHINING STAR
HE TELLS ME THIS IS LOVE, AND THAT'S TOO FAR
FAR FROM THE VOW HE TOOK IN FAITH TO
PROTECT
THOSE VOWS HAVE TURNED TO SHAME AND
TO REGRET

TAKE AWAY THE WALLS SURROUNDING ME
MANY RUN AWAY AFRAID OF WHAT THEY'LL BE
CAN'T YOU COME IN CLOSE AND HOLD ME
TIGHT, LORD
CAN'T YOU HEAR ME CRYING IN THE NIGHT,
LORD
TAKE AWAY THIS PAIN INSIDE OF ME
RUN AWAY, WE'RE RUNNING TO BE FREE

> *The door to the cellar opens. JULIA stands frozen with hands behind her back. FATHER CHRISTOPHER enters and stands in the doorway.*

FATHER: I came to make sure you hadn't run again. How many did you get?

> *He grabs her arms and holds up her hands. He kisses her fingers.*

My little princess.

JULIA: Don't.

JULIA takes her hands away.

FATHER: If you stop running, no one will hurt you. The world out there doesn't know what's best for you but I do. It's here with me. I can protect you. *(Pause.)* Come here.

JULIA shakes her head "no."

Come here.

After a moment FATHER CHRISTOPHER goes to JULIA, as SISTER BERNADETTE enters the room and stands frozen. He takes off JULIA's dress and they lie down together. After a moment, SISTER BERNADETTE turns and shuts the door. FATHER CHRISTOPHER gets up to put his robe on. He exits. JULIA turns and sits on the edge of the bed wrapped in a blanket.

JULIA: ASK FOR FORGIVENESS, I CAN'T DEFEND
PRAY FOR FORGIVENESS, AND COME AN END
GOD-LOVING MAN TOOK MY INNOCENCE
AND I HOPE FOR THE DAY THAT I CAN

TAKE AWAY THE WALLS SURROUNDING ME
MANY RUN AWAY AFRAID OF WHAT THEY'LL BE
CAN'T YOU COME IN CLOSE AND HOLD ME TIGHT, LORD
CAN'T YOU HEAR ME CRYING IN THE NIGHT, LORD
TAKE AWAY THIS PAIN INSIDE OF ME
RUN AWAY, WE'RE RUNNING TO BE FREE

Scene 9

> *In the cellar, it is night and very dark. WILSON is heard doing his best wolf howl. He enters the cellar followed by JOANNA and ELIZABETH.*

WILSON: All in!

JULIA: What? What are you doing here?

JOANNA: You thought we'd leave you here all alone?

JULIA: What about the bed count? Sister is going to be double-checking, I'm sure.

ELIZABETH: We stayed in bed until she checked twice.

JULIA: But how were you able to come together?

> *JOANNA grabs the* Alice in Wonderland *book from ELIZABETH's hands.*

JOANNA: We've been using this Wonderland book, sending it back and forth. Folding down the top corner of the page and circling the words to make a message. Easy.

> *Movement is heard outside the door.*

JULIA: You hear that?

WILSON: The best part.

> *TOMMY and VINCENT fly through the door with a large sack full of food.*

TOMMY: Hope you're hungry.

VINCENT: Straight from the staff kitchen.

JULIA: I didn't know when I would get to see you again.

> *JULIA and TOMMY hug, and JULIA holds on extra-long.*

TOMMY: I'm here. Not going anywhere.

JULIA: You are just the first faces I've seen all week.

JOANNA: Well, we've come prepared. Here, sit, eat.

> *JOANNA and ELIZABETH have taken food out
> and prepared it in a circle. They've stretched out
> a blanket for them to sit on. WILSON grabs the
> letter from TOMMY's pocket.*

TOMMY: Give those back!

WILSON: Oh, come on. This is all you've been doing for
               days.

VINCENT: Can we read it?

TOMMY: No. I wanted Julia to read it...

> *WILSON points to a spot on the page.*

WILSON: A Chief! You're writing to a Chief! Tommy,
               I didn't know you were a rebel.

> *VINCENT imitates FATHER CHRISTOPHER.*

VINCENT: This kind of writing is unacceptable!

> *VINCENT takes the page, rolls it up, and hits
> WILSON over the head with it. WILSON takes
> the page and holds it above his head. WILSON
> does his best FATHER CHRISTOPHER imitation.*

WILSON: Pray for your sins, you dirty Indian.

> *VINCENT laughs. TOMMY runs to grab the
> page from WILSON's hands but misses.*

WILSON & VINCENT: Scrub the brown out!

> *They scrub their arms and laugh.*

TOMMY: Don't be an ass.

WILSON: What are you doing with this, huh?

TOMMY: Nothing! It's stupid, I shouldn't have written it.

WILSON: Do you know what they're gonna do to you if
               they find this?

VINCENT: I bet they'd shave your head.

WILSON: No, for this? They'd have you lead the pee parade...

VINCENT: Uhhhh, that's disgusting. With someone else's pissed sheets on your head?

TOMMY: Shut up.

JULIA: Read it, please.

WILSON: You're all tough on paper but deep down you're a chicken. And what a good student! You even put your name and date at the top of the first page. Read, or I'll slip it under Father Christopher's door...

TOMMY: You wouldn't.

WILSON: Watch me.

WILSON slowly walks toward the door holding out the page.

TOMMY: *(Pause.)* OK!

ALL: Yes!

WILSON walks over to TOMMY and presses the page into his chest.

WILSON: I knew you'd listen to reason.

TOMMY: If I read this, it stays between us. If word gets out about any of this I'll be lucky to get the pee parade.

WILSON: OK, go on.

TOMMY: I don't even know if I got all the words right. I was sounding it out and making up the spelling.

ELIZABETH: I want to hear you speak Ojibway.

JOANNA: *Boogidi dibishko makwa.* He farts like a bear.

All laugh.

JULIA: We won't tell anyone.

VINCENT: Tommy, the REBEL!

              All laugh.

TOMMY: OK, OK. You guys make me crazy. *(Pause.)* For
              Julia.

GIMIKWENDEN INA
(Do you remember?)

GIMIKWENDEN INA (Do you remember?)
AANIIN EZHINIKAAZOYAN (What you are called)
AANDI WENJIBAAYAN (Where you are from)
GIMIKWENDEN INA (Do you remember?)

GIMIKWENDEN INA (Do you remember?)
NINDEDEYAG NIMAAMAAYAG (Our fathers and
mothers)
NIMISEYAG NISAYEYAH (Our sisters and brothers)
DO YOU HEAR THEM CALLING YOU?

BOYS: *GIMIKWENDEN INA*

GIRLS: DO YOU REMEMBER

BOYS: *NINDEDEYAG NIMAAMAAYAG*

GIRLS: OUR FATHERS AND MOTHERS

BOYS: *NIMISEYAG NISAYEYAH*

GIRLS: OUR SISTERS AND BROTHERS

ALL: DO YOU HEAR THEM CALLING YOU?

              *They begin handing out the food and gifts.
              JOANNA holds up a red flower necklace and
              gives it to JULIA. TOMMY takes it and puts
              it around her neck. He lies on her lap. They
              are eating and laughing together under their
              singing.*

GIRLS: AHHHH…

BOYS: YAH HEY YAH WAY HEY YA HAH

GIRLS: AHHHH…

BOYS: YAH HEY YAH WAY HEY YA HAH

GIRLS: AHHHH…

BOYS: YAH HEY YAH WAY HEY YA HAH

GIRLS: AHHHH…

> *A drum is heard off in the distance as RITA appears as a vision behind the children, who are in awe. RITA is holding a drum and begins to sing, teaching the children this song.*

RITA: HI YEAH HI YEAH HI YAH YAH
            HI YEAH HI YEAH HI YAH YAH
            HI YEAH HI YEAH HI YAH YAH YAH
            HI YEAH HI YEAH HI YAH

RITA, JULIA, TOMMY:
            HI YEAH HI YEAH HI YAH YAH
            HI YEAH HI YEAH HI YAH YAH
            HI YEAH HI YEAH HI YAH YAH YAH
            HI YEAH HI YEAH HI YAH

> *They take the sheet they were sitting on off the floor and stretch it out into a large drum. They spin around it, drumming and singing. RITA begins dancing and then they all join her. They take the sheets off the bed and dance around with them as shawls.*

ALL: HI YEAH HI YEAH HI YAH YAH
            HI YEAH HI YEAH HI YAH YAH
            HI YEAH HI YEAH HI YAH YAH YAH
            HI YEAH HI YEAH HI YAH

            HI YEAH HI YEAH HI YAH YAH
            HI YEAH HI YEAH HI YAH YAH
            HI YEAH HI YEAH HI YAH YAH YAH
            HI YEAH HI YEAH HI YAH

HI YEAH HI YEAH HI YAH YAH
HI YEAH HI YEAH HI YAH YAH
HI YEAH HI YEAH HI YAH YAH YAH
HI YEAH HI YEAH HI YAH

Only drum and voices echo.

HI YEAH HI YEAH HI YAH YAH
HI YEAH HI YEAH HI YAH YAH
HI YEAH HI YEAH HI YAH YAH YAH
HI YEAH HI YEAH HI YAH

Voices build wildly and unhinged movement from all in a circular motion around TOMMY and WILSON as their younger selves, transforming into their older selves, with the memories of their younger selves dancing and singing around them.

Scene 10

<u>THIS IS WHAT YOU GET</u>

TOM & WILSON: *(Overlapping.)*
TAKE IT BACK, CAN WE GO BACK?
I'LL TAKE IT BACK AND START ALL OVER.
TAKE IT BACK, CAN WE GO BACK?
I'LL TAKE IT BACK AND START ALL OVER.

ALL: *(Overlapping.)*
HI YEAH HI YEAH HI YAH YAH
HI YEAH HI YEAH HI YAH YAH
HI YEAH HI YEAH HI YAH YAH YAH
HI YEAH HI YEAH HI YAH

> *All other cast members circle TOM and WILSON, then disappear into the distance still dancing and singing.*

TAKE IT BACK, CAN WE GO BACK?
I'LL TAKE IT BACK AND START ALL OVER.
TAKE IT BACK, CAN WE GO BACK?
I'LL TAKE IT BACK AND START ALL OVER.

> *All cast exit except JULIA and RITA, who are watching TOM from a distance. JULIA and RITA exit.*

TOM: TONIGHT WE'RE BACK TO WHERE WE STARTED,
THE PAST WE'RE TRYING TO FORGET,
WE'RE HERE AS IF WE CAN RESOLVE IT,
I'LL SHOW YOU, THIS IS WHAT YOU GET.

> *Back to WILSON and TOM at the bar; several drinks later.*

WILSON: Tom, I'm not looking to start a fight.

TOM: You may have beat me back in school, but I guarantee you I can kick your ass today.

WILSON: I had no idea…

TOM: What do you wanna know, huh? That I'm a drunk? I was sober for three months until today. Bet you didn't know that, smartass! Too bad that suit and tie don't buy street smarts.

WILSON: I know that what happened must have fucked you up.

TOM: I'm mad twenty-three hours of the day. That's all I've known.

WILSON: Tom, I'm serious when I tell you: you need help!

TOM: Maybe you should have thought of that before beating the shit out of me all through Indian school.

WILSON: How was I supposed to know what was going to happen?

TAKE IT BACK, CAN WE GO BACK?
I'LL TAKE IT BACK AND START ALL OVER.

WILSON, JULIA, SISTER BERNADETTE:
TAKE IT BACK, CAN WE GO BACK?
I'LL TAKE IT BACK AND START ALL OVER.

> *In the cellar, JULIA is throwing up in a bucket. SISTER is frazzled, throwing Julia's clothes into a small bag.*

JULIA: Sister, you believe me?

SISTER: I do.

JULIA: What's happening to me?

SISTER: Stop asking that! Have you told anyone else?

JULIA: About Father Christopher or... (*Pause.*) No, I haven't.

SISTER: Oh good. We need to see the Monsignor at once.

WE'LL NEED TO SEND YOU AWAY

JULIA: WHERE DO I GO, I HAVE NOWHERE TO GO.

SISTER: THERE'S NO OPTION TO STAY

JULIA: WHERE WILL I GO, BUT THE OTHERS DON'T
               KNOW.

               *SISTER ties up JULIA's small bag and puts a
               sweater on her.*

JULIA, SISTER BERNADETTE, WILSON:
               TONIGHT I'M BEGGING TO BE PARDONED
               FOR THINGS I DID THAT I REGRET
               YOUR FACE, ONCE FRIENDLY, NOW HAS
               HARDENED
               AND SHOWN ME, THIS IS WHAT YOU GET

               *SISTER and JULIA leave the cellar. RITA is
               coming down the path to the front gate of the
               school.*

WILSON, TOM, SISTER, JULIA, RITA:
               TAKE IT BACK, CAN WE GO BACK?
               I'LL TAKE IT BACK AND START ALL OVER.
               TAKE IT BACK, CAN WE GO BACK?
               I'LL TAKE IT BACK AND START ALL OVER.

               *RITA arrives at the gate and meets SISTER
               BERNADETTE, who puts her hand out to
               stop her.*

SISTER: Stop! We cannot allow you past this gate, you're
               not allowed to be here. You know that.

RITA: THEY DIDN'T GIVE ME A CHOICE,
               I WAS HELPLESS TO STOP IT ALL

SISTER: The children are in English lessons, doing very
               well, and we feel that if they are exposed to
               Indians outside of school they will fall back to
               their old ways. And you don't want that.

RITA: YOU HAD TO GO, HAD TO GO,
               YOU KNEW STAYING WAS AGAINST THE LAW

SISTER: If you fill out the paperwork, you can visit your
               children.

RITA: I can't read this.

TOM & JULIA: WHY DID YOU SEND US AWAY?

RITA: THEY DIDN'T GIVE ME A CHOICE,
             I WAS HELPLESS TO STOP IT ALL

TOM & JULIA: NOW WE'RE LOSING OUR WAY

RITA: YOU HAD TO GO, HAD TO GO,
             YOU KNEW STAYING WAS AGAINST THE LAW

> *RITA exits.*

> *SISTER BERNADETTE ushers JULIA through the dark hallways of the school secretly to the Monsignor's office door, where FATHER CHRISTOPHER steps out and surprises them, then shuts the door behind him.*

FATHER: What is the matter?

SISTER: Father, I need to talk to Monsignor. Please, excuse me!

FATHER: Sister, you know the chain of command. You come to me, and I will decide if we need to involve Monsignor.

SISTER: You've done enough already.

FATHER: SISTER, YOU CAN'T TAKE THESE ACCUSATIONS SERIOUSLY

> *At the bar, WILSON gets up to leave.*

TOM: I'll beat your fucking head right into the ground.

FATHER: AFTER ALL, SHE'S A RUNNER

WILSON: We were stupid kids.

FATHER: YOU CAN'T TAKE HER WORD ON THIS SO EASILY

SISTER: Father, it's different this time.

FATHER: CHILDREN MAKE UP THESE LIES ABOUT STAFF

SISTER: I believe her.

FATHER: AND WHAT PROOF DO YOU HAVE?

SISTER: She's pregnant.

WILSON: It happened to us too. I was beaten, abused, had those fuckers crawl into my bed and did to me ten times worse than whatever happened to you.

> *SISTER BERNADETTE knocks frantically on Monsignor's door.*

SISTER: Monsignor! I'm sorry to bother you like this. Please, this is important.

TOM & FATHER: Shut up! Shut up!

> *FATHER grabs SISTER BERNADETTE and pulls her away from the door and throws her across the hall. She screams. TOM grabs WILSON and throws him across the bar.*

ALL CAST: TAKE IT BACK, CAN WE GO BACK?
            I'LL TAKE IT BACK AND START ALL OVER.
            TAKE IT BACK, CAN WE GO BACK?
            I'LL TAKE IT BACK AND START ALL OVER.

FATHER: SEND FOR THE DOCTOR IN TOWN

JULIA: WHY DO I NEED A DOCTOR ANYHOW?

SISTER: Don't touch her!

FATHER: YOU WILL GO AGAINST GOD?

SISTER: BUT HE SHOULD KNOW,
            WE SHOULD TELL MONSIGNOR RIGHT AWAY

FATHER: Sister, place Julia in solitary confinement until the doctor comes this evening.

SISTER: No!

JULIA: Why do I need a doctor?

SISTER: We need Monsignor's permission before sending her…

FATHER: …An Indian girl with a child will be damned to hell. Do you want her to survive or not? If she has this baby she will die. We have to protect her. This is protocol, Monsignor would say the same.

> *SISTER BERNADETTE shakes her head "no" and backs away as FATHER CHRISTOPHER pulls JULIA down the hallway.*

ALL CAST: TAKE IT BACK, CAN WE GO BACK?
I TAKE IT BACK AND START ALL OVER.
TAKE IT BACK, CAN WE GO BACK?
I TAKE IT BACK AND START ALL OVER.

SISTER & FATHER: *(Overlapping.)*
TONIGHT WE ALTER WHAT WAS STARTED,
THE PAST WE'RE TRYING TO FORGET,
TONIGHT, ATTEMPTING TO RESOLVE IT,
AND SHOW YOU, THIS IS WHAT YOU GET.

TOM, JULIA, WILSON, VINCENT, JOANNA, ELIZABETH:
(Overlapping.)
WHY DID YOU SEND US AWAY?

RITA: THEY DIDN'T GIVE ME A CHOICE,
I WAS HELPLESS TO STOP IT ALL

TOM, JULIA, WILSON, VINCENT, JOANNA, ELIZABETH:
NOW WE'RE LOSING OUR WAY

RITA: YOU HAD TO GO, HAD TO GO,
YOU KNEW STAYING WAS AGAINST THE LAW

TOM, JULIA, WILSON, VINCENT, JOANNA, ELIZABETH & RITA:
TAKE AWAY THE WALLS SURROUNDING ME
MANY RUN AWAY, WE'RE RUNNING TO BE FREE.

ALL *(Except WILSON)*:
TAKE IT BACK, CAN WE GO BACK?
I'LL TAKE IT BACK AND START ALL OVER.
TAKE IT BACK, CAN WE GO BACK?
I'LL TAKE IT BACK AND START ALL OVER.

WILSON:	(*Overlapping with section above.*) You're not worth my fucking time. I'm trying to help you. You were better off, you got out. Vincent and I…

VINCENT appears to WILSON in a vision.

VINCENT:	WE'RE FALLING BUT WE WILL NOT TOUCH THE GROUND
WILSON:	We weren't so lucky.
VINCENT:	THEY SENT US HERE AND THIS IS WHAT WE'VE FOUND
WILSON:	He was the same as you, angry, aggressive, couldn't keep his life together.
VINCENT:	NOW ALL THEY SAY IS FORCING ITS WAY DOWN
WILSON:	Ten years ago,
VINCENT:	WE RUN AWAY, WE'RE RUNNING TO THE SOUND.
WILSON:	Vincent shot himself in the head.

VINCENT disappears into darkness.

I'm sorry for trying to save you from what happened to him.

ALL:	TONIGHT WE ALTER WHAT WAS STARTED, THE PAST WE'RE TRYING TO FORGET, TONIGHT, ATTEMPTING TO RESOLVE IT, AND SHOW YOU, AND SHOW YOU, AND SHOW YOU, AND SHOW YOU, AND SHOW YOU, AND SHOW YOU, AND SHOW YOU THIS IS WHAT YOU GET.

End of Act One.

Act Two

Scene 1

> *In the Boys' Dorm, WILSON, VINCENT, and TOMMY enter, running to their beds. They sit on their knees as they watch* The Lone Ranger *and bounce in excitement to the song.*

AWAY WE RIDE

WILSON: BARUM BARUM BARUM BA BA

TOMMY: BA BA BA

VINCENT: BA BA BA

BOYS: BARUM BARUM BARUM BUM BUM
              BARUM BARUM BARUM BUM BUM
              BARUM BARUM BARUM BUM BUM
              BARUM BARUM BUM BUM

WILSON: TAKE A RIDE TO WHEREVER

BOYS: HI OH!

WILSON: THAT WHITE STALLION WILL FLY

BOYS: HI OH!

WILSON: EVIL BANDITS WILL NEVER

BOYS: HI OH!

WILSON: THEY BETTER NOT EVEN TRY

BOYS: SILVER AWAY!

> *Boys take the* Alice in Wonderland *book, and begin circling words. WILSON sneaks outside and hides it under a tree for the girls to find. FATHER CHRISTOPHER is in his office.*

FATHER CHRISTOPHER:
> GOD IN HEAVEN ANSWER ME,
> CAN'T YOU EVEN TRY
> I CONFESS TO ALL YOU SEE,
> WITHOUT A REASON WHY
> I WAS HAD TOO YOUNG, I WAS HAD LIKE HER
> IF THERE'S BLAME TO LAY, THEN LAY IT ON
> IF THERE'S BLAME TO LAY, THEN LAY IT ON
> THEM ON THEM
> GOD IN HEAVEN ANSWER ME,
> CAN'T YOU EVEN TRY.

> *JOANNA and ELIZABETH are cleaning the floors.*

ELIZABETH: You have to ask, it's been weeks since we've seen her.

JOANNA: Sister will never tell us.

ELIZABETH: She wasn't in the cellar when we checked. Do you think she ran again?

JOANNA: Maybe she made it this time.

ELIZABETH: We should check our hiding spot and see if the boys have left word for us.

> *SISTER BERNADETTE enters with a basin of water for JULIA.*

JOANNA: Sister, we haven't seen Julia in weeks...

SISTER: She ran again. Back to work.

> *SISTER exits. Back to the boys.*

WILSON: I'm the cowboy, and you're the Indians.

VINCENT: No way!

TOMMY: Why?

WILSON: Because I said so! That's why.

            They run around making horse and gunshot noises.

VINCENT: (*Overlapping.*)
            BARUM BARUM BARUM BUM BUM
            BARUM BARUM BARUM BUM BUM
            BARUM BARUM BARUM BUM BUM
            BARUM BARUM BUM BUM

            VINCENT jumps on TOMMY's back and rides him like a horse. WILSON is standing on the bed bouncing and holding the reins of the horse.

WILSON: FAR ALONG THE HORIZON

TOMMY: HI OH!

WILSON: I WILL MEET YOU THERE

TOMMY: HI OH!

WILSON: A FREE SPIRIT TO GLIDE ON

TOMMY: HI OH!

WILSON: WITHOUT A SINGLE CARE

BOYS: SILVER AWAY!

TOMMY: AWAY WE RIDE!

VINCENT: AWAY WE RIDE!

WILSON: AWAY WE RIDE!

FATHER CHRISTOPHER:
>GOD IN HEAVEN MERCY PLEASE,
>RID ME OF THIS GUILT
>I NEVER MEANT TO LET IT GET THIS FAR,
>A SIN FROM WHAT YOU BUILT
>LOST ALL SELF-CONTROL,
>LOST YOUR HONOUR BUT
>WALK AROUND THIS JAIL FOR SEVEN YEARS
>AND SEE WHERE YOU,
>LET'S SEE WHERE YOU STEER?
>WHERE YOU GO?
>I'M NOT SURE IT'S MEANT FOR ME
>I'M NOT SURE AT ALL.

JOANNA: There it is!

> *JOANNA and ELIZABETH run to the book hidden under a tree. They open a book, search for the folded-down corner, and find the message from the boys.*

ELIZABETH: Here's the message. OK, of course they would choose that part.

JOANNA: They're gross.

ELIZABETH: They say she's in Bernie's private cabin.

JOANNA: Are they hiding her?

ELIZABETH: It says Tommy's going to sneak out tonight after everyone's in bed to see her.

JOANNA: Bernie lied.

> *They grab their bucket and run into the school. Boys circle the beds making gunshot noises.*

WILSON: I killed you!

VINCENT: No, you didn't!

WILSON loads an imaginary shotgun and makes a gunshot sound pointing at VINCENT's head.

WILSON: There, now you're dead!

VINCENT drops to the ground, enthusiastically. The boys gallop riding horses around their dorm.

TAKE A RIDE TO WHEREVER

BOYS: HI OH!

WILSON: THAT WHITE STALLION WILL FLY

BOYS: HI OH!

WILSON: EVIL BANDITS WILL NEVER

BOYS: HI OH!

WILSON: THEY BETTER NOT EVEN TRY

BOYS: SILVER AWAY!

ALL BOYS: BARUM BARUM BARUM BUM BUM
            BARUM BARUM BARUM BUM BUM
            BARUM BARUM BARUM BUM BUM
            BARUM BARUM BUM BUM
            AWAY WE RIDE!

The boys sit on the bed as FATHER CHRIS-TOPHER appears in the doorway behind them.

FATHER: Tommy, follow me, please.

BOYS: Uh, oh.

TOMMY: Shut it.

FATHER CHRISTOPHER escorts TOMMY to his office where there is a small fireplace. FATHER is holding the papers with TOMMY's writing on them.

FATHER: Tommy, I saw what you wrote. You are aware this is the devil's work.

> *TOMMY nods "yes."*

This is the type of behaviour that takes away everything we have been working towards. We are trying to make you better, so that you will have a future in our society. But what you've done will only hold us back in our efforts. Do you want us to help you?

TOMMY: Yes.

FATHER: Then you promise me, right now. Never use this kind of gibberish ever again.

TOMMY: I promise.

FATHER: Good. I will decide a suitable punishment for you later. But now I want you to take each page, and burn it. The fire will only remove the physical writing, but it is up to you to erase the rest from your mind. Then you may ask the Lord to forgive you.

> *TOMMY holds the first paper up above the fire and lets it drop. They exit.*

> *Transition into Act Two Scene 2 (music).*

Scene 2

> *In SISTER BERNADETTE's private cabin, JULIA is in bed. SISTER enters with a bucket of water. JULIA is sick; she has had an operation and is recovering slowly. SISTER opens the curtains and walks over towards the bedside table where JULIA's lunch is sitting, untouched.*

SISTER: Julia? I've brought you some things to get yourself cleaned up. How are you supposed to get better if you won't even touch your food?

JULIA: I'm not hungry.

SISTER: You must eat. The sooner you do, the sooner you can be back with your classmates.

JULIA: I've been starved for weeks. Now that I'm sick you want me to eat?

SISTER: Well...you want to be well.

JULIA: This is all I've ever known. I can't even imagine a world away from here.

SISTER: We have no idea what God has planned for us.

JULIA: God? All I ever hear about is God. You all keep talking about him. Where is he? He has abandoned me like my father and mother.

> *JULIA throws her tray of food on the floor.*

SISTER: Watch your mouth! How dare you talk to me in that tone of voice. I'm trying to help you! (*Pause.*) These are times when we need God most. When we have made a mistake, lost the path, or sinned; he will forgive when others turn their backs. Allow him to forgive you for your sins; take responsibility for your part in this and start anew.

GOD ONLY KNOWS (reprise)

SISTER: *(Pause.)* I know it's a scary place. But with prayer and discipline, you can have a new life. Have faith, Julia. I will be back later this evening and I expect your food to be eaten.

> *SISTER leaves JULIA in the cabin and stops on the porch.*

LORD GIVE ME THE STRENGTH I FEAR THE FALL
LORD I FEEL SHAMEFUL FROM IT ALL
TAKE AWAY DOUBTS INSIDE MY HEAD
ALLOW ME TO FOLLOW WHERE I'M LED

THEY WARNED ME THAT THESE SCHOOLS
WERE HARSH AND WILD
THEY SAID TO TAKE THE INDIAN OUT OF THE
CHILD
BUT ALL I'VE DONE IN FEAR I'VE GROWN TO
HATE
PLEASE ANSWER MY PRAYER, I WILL AWAIT

GOD ONLY KNOWS WHAT WE'VE BEEN
THROUGH
IF HE COULD SEE US WHAT WOULD HE DO
GOD ONLY KNOWS HOW MUCH WE TAKE
HE ALONE SEES US WHEN WE BREAK.

> *On the street outside the bar TOM, drunk, lunges at WILSON, who ducks out of the way.*

WHEN WE BREAK, WE BREAK

WILSON: What is this? You wanna fight me?

TOM: I wouldn't wanna wrinkle your suit.

SISTER: GOD ONLY SEES US WHEN WE BREAK

WILSON: Someday you're gonna have to talk about her.

> *TOM grabs WILSON by the lapels and gets in his face.*

TOM:	Shut up! Shut up!

| SISTER: | WHEN WE BREAK, WE'LL BREAK |

WILSON pushes TOM away.

| WILSON: | Will you just listen to me. |

| SISTER: | WHEN WE BREAK. |

SISTER BERNADETTE exits.

WILSON: GOD ONLY KNOWS WHAT WE'VE BEEN
THROUGH
IF HE COULD SEE US WHAT WOULD HE DO
GOD ONLY KNOWS HOW MUCH WE TAKE
HE ALONE SEES US WHEN WE BREAK.

I wish that I had talked to Vincent when he started acting like you. What would Julia say if she saw you now?

| ALL CAST: | WHEN WE BREAK, WE BREAK |

| WILSON: | IF SHE COULD SEE YA, WHAT WOULD SHE DO? |

ALL CAST (*Except WILSON and TOM*):
GOD ONLY SEES US WHEN WE BREAK

| WILSON: | Anyways. I'm no expert on these things. |

ALL CAST (*Except WILSON and TOM*):
WHEN WE BREAK,

| WILSON: | Go home, Tom. |

| ALL CAST: | WE'LL BREAK |

TOM exits.

| WILSON: | WHEN WE BREAK. |

WILSON exits. TOMMY appears suddenly and sneaks into the cabin.

| JULIA: | Tommy! How did you know where to find me? |

TOMMY: I know every inch of this school. I saw Sister leave. We don't have much time.

JULIA: What's that mark on your face? Have those boys been beating on you?

TOMMY: It doesn't matter now. Let's get out of here.

JULIA: No.

TOMMY: What did they do to you?

JULIA: I don't know. The floor was bright red from my insides.

TOMMY: Is that why they have you in Bernie's cabin?

JULIA: She tells me to eat and get better. But if getting better means living that all over again? I don't think I can.

TOMMY: Hey, don't talk like that. We're stronger together. If we leave now, we will never come back or feel this way again.

JULIA: Tommy, I can't do it.

TOMMY: Tomorrow, we'll run tomorrow.

THE CLOSEST THING TO HOME (reprise)

The two of us will be able to find our way home. It's no fun going alone anyways.

TOMMY: WE'LL BE THE FIRST ONES TO MAKE IT OUT
THEY'LL SPREAD THE WORD FOREVER
WE'LL BE SAFE AT HOME FAR AWAY,
WE WON'T LOOK BACK
IF YOU GET TIRED WE'LL TAKE A BREAK
I KNOW IT WILL BE BETTER
THOSE YEARS WE HAVE DREAMED ABOUT
ARE READY TO COME TRUE

THEY SAY WE SHOULD FORGET IT ALL
THEY SAY IT ALL MAKES US BAD
THESE MEMORIES WE WON'T OUTGROW
AND YOU'RE THE CLOSEST THING TO HOME
I KNOW.

I heard about these kids whose parents wouldn't let them be taken to school. Their parents took all the kids and hid them in this cabin deep in the woods and guarded the place with shotguns. When the police found out where they were and came with the Monsignor, they heard gunshots! They turned around and left them alone. Can you believe it? Those kids got to stay with their parents. When we find *Nimaamaa*, I bet she'll do that for us.

JULIA: Maybe.

TOMMY: I will be back here, and we'll go. I'll stash some food away and find you a walking stick to help you out. Will you come?

I REMEMBER ALL OF IT STILL
I CAN SEE YOU RUNNING UP OUR HILL
I CAN HEAR THOSE DRUMS BEAT
I CAN FEEL THE GROUND TOUCH MY BARE FEET

THE CLOSEST THING TO LIFE
THE CLOSEST THING TO HOME
YOU'RE THE CLOSEST THING TO LOVE I KNOW

JULIA: Yeah, Tommy. Tomorrow, OK?

TOMMY starts to leave but JULIA holds out her arms for a hug, TOMMY goes to her but gives her a noogie instead. They laugh and he exits. She sits on the end of the bed looking out the window.

HOMEWARD BOUND

I PACK MY BAG WITH ALL MY THINGS
AND SNEAK DOWN THE HALLS
THE MOULDINGS UP ABOVE CARVED ANGEL
WINGS ON THE WALLS

AS I REACH THE WOODEN DOOR,
I LOOK BACK JUST MAKING SURE
BUT IF YOU LIFT UP SLIGHTLY,
IT DOESN'T MAKE MUCH SOUND
AND I SLIDE THROUGH THE CRACK
SURE THAT NO ONE IS AROUND

AND I CRAWL PAST THE TRICKY SPOT
THE PLACE ALL THE KIDS GET CAUGHT
AND I MAKE IT OVER TO THE FAR SIDE OF THE
FIELD
I JUMP THE FENCE AND PUT MY BAG UP AS A
SHIELD

AND I TURN RIGHT, THE ANISHNAABE WAY,
MA WOULD SAY
I'M IN A FIELD OF FLOWERS BRIGHTLY RED,
WILDLY SPREAD

I FALL BACK ON THEM AND SMILE
MAKE SNOW ANGELS FOR A WHILE
THEN I PICK A FEW, AND PUT THEM IN MY SACK
A SIGN FROM THE CREATOR, THAT I'M NEVER
COMING BACK

AND I TAKE THE ROAD I REMEMBER
FOLLOW IT RIGHT INTO TOWN
HOP ON BACK OF THE TRAIN THAT'S HEADING
HOMEWARD BOUND

HOME WHERE PEOPLE WILL KNOW ME
HOME WHERE PEOPLE WILL HELP
PA SAID WALKING WILL DO YOU GOOD
BACK WHERE PEOPLE ACT LIKE THEY SHOULD

AND THERE IT IS
THE TREE TOMMY AND I CARVED OUR
INITIALS INTO

I KNOW MY WAY FROM HERE
TOMMY AND I CAN RUN THIS TRAIL WITH
OUR EYES CLOSED
KNOWING EVERY STEP TO DODGE THE ROOTS
AND BRANCHES
KNOWING WHEN YOU DUCK TO GUARD YOUR
EYES
MA AND PA WILL RUN TO MEET ME ARMS
WIDE OPEN
ON THE DOOR I KNOCK WITH ALL MY MIGHT

She stands up.

Hey, *Niin abi!* (I'm home!) *Nimaamaa!* (Mother!) *Nindede!* (Father!)... I'm home! Maybe they're in the back yard. Ma... Pa...it's *gidaanis!* (your daughter!) I'll wait for them. (*Long pause.*) They're gone. No one came for us and no one comes.

Scene 3

> *In RITA's living room, the TV is flickering. RITA is sitting on a chair watching in the dark as TOM enters quietly, trying not to be heard. He sneaks past her in the dark.*

RITA: Hold it!

TOM: 'night.

RITA: Not so fast. Who do you think you are, sneaking into my house in the middle of the night?

TOM: It's not what it looks like. I lost track of time and ended up staying out way too late.

RITA: For Christ's sake, Tom. I've been sitting here worried about you for hours.

TOM: I got busy.

RITA: Busy? Did you even make it to the interview?

TOM: Yeah, I got it. I'll be out of here for good. Happy?

RITA: You lying sack of shit.

TOM: I don't wanna talk about it.

RITA: I'm not having a son running around in the middle of the night doing God knows what.

TOM: Ma, you don't need to wait up.

RITA: I'm setting down the ground rules for the house.

TOM: What? Now you're gonna be a parent to me?

RITA: Don't give me that shit.

TOM: About time, eh?

RITA: I'm your Mother…

TOM: And a hell of a job you've done.

RITA: How do I know you're not lying dead in a ditch somewhere, huh?

TOM: I'm under your roof so I got to follow your rules? You sound like them.

RITA: I sound like who?

TOM: Ma, I'm not doing this.

RITA: You been drinkin' again? I tell 'em I won't do it again…

TOM: I haven't been drinking!

RITA: Bullshit. I want you to leave here tonight. I don't care anymore!

TOM: I fucked up! I did, but will you just wait a Goddamn minute, please? I lost it, for a second I saw red… I saw him…an'…fuck it, you wouldn't get it anyways. (Pause.)

I went to school with him, an'…

Ugh, you know, I haven't felt that way in so long. Seeing him there doing so well, living his life as if nothing happened, as if that place hadn't changed us forever.

I couldn't take it.

RITA: What did you do?

TOM: He wanted me to talk about her.

RITA: Who?

TOM: You don't like it when I talk bad about school.

HOMEWARD BOUND
(instrumental)

Scene 4

> *Young WILSON and VINCENT enter running.*

WILSON & VINCENT:
> There he is!

WILSON: Vince, grab him!

> *They grab TOM and throw him across the room, transforming TOM into his younger self, with every kick.*

TOMMY: What? Wait. Come on, guys.

> *TOMMY is thrown down, falling to his knees. WILSON punches TOMMY in the stomach and kicks him in the face.*

VINCENT: They're making us lead the pee parade.

WILSON: For lying about your letter.

> *WILSON and VINCENT are circling TOMMY. WILSON kicks TOMMY on the ground as VINCENT removes his belt and begins whipping him on the back with it.*

TOMMY: I told you what would happen.

VINCENT: We didn't write it, though. You did.

WILSON: Why should we take the punishment for your stupid shit...

> *VINCENT grabs TOMMY's arms and holds him up facing WILSON. TOMMY lets out a cry. WILSON pushes TOMMY to the ground then spits on him. FATHER CHRISTOPHER enters with a hose. The boys stop.*

TOMMY: Father, help!

> *WILSON and VINCENT grab TOMMY and hold him up with his arms out to the sides.*

Whoa, wait! I've gotta get to Julia!

FATHER: You deliberately disobeyed me.

TOMMY: No. I burned the papers, they're all gone. I have nothing else.

FATHER: You must be punished. How else will you learn?

TOMMY: I promise! I promise I will never do it again.

FATHER: Good.

> *FATHER CHRISTOPHER hoses TOMMY, soaking him. TOMMY cries out in pain.*

WILSON: Vince, hold him down!

VINCENT: I'm tryin'!

TOMMY: Please! (*Coughs, choking on the water.*) STOP!

> *WILSON and VINCENT throw him to the ground and run off. After a moment TOMMY is alone, on the floor in the fetal position; coughing and crying in pain. TOMMY stands, stumbling toward SISTER BERNADETTE's cabin. In the light streaming in from the window is JULIA's silhouette hanging by one of the chains from the swing set.*

Julia?

> *He searches the room frantically.*

Oh no.

> *He approaches the open window.*

Help!

> *SISTER enters.*

SISTER: What are you doing in here? Where is…

She looks out the window.

Julia!

SISTER runs to the doorway.

Monsignor! Get the children into the main hall now!

TOMMY collapses at the foot of her bed. SISTER blows her whistle in a panic and she leaves the cabin. Her whistle echoes off in the distance as TOM stands watching the memory fade.

RITA: They told me she ran away.

TOM: She was just hanging there.

RITA: That's…that's not my girl you're talking about…

TOM: I should have carried her…she couldn't walk when I wanted to run the day before.

RITA: Wh… Why didn't you tell me before?

TOM: They told us not to tell.

RITA: You're lying…you lie.

TOM: I wish. I wish she had run away. That she had made it. And then…then there would be a chance I could see her again.

RITA cries out. TOM doesn't move. After a moment of silence:

PATER NOSTER (reprise)

SISTER BERNADETTE enters as RITA exits. TOM exits. SISTER BERNADETTE goes to the bed, and picks up the clothes as JOANNA and ELIZABETH enter and pack up Julia's things and exit.

Scene 5

In the chapel, the Children, except JULIA and TOMMY, walk in line with their heads down. They don't look at one another. They are followed only by FATHER CHRISTOPHER.

STUDENTS & FATHER CHRISTOPHER:
Mm...

PATER NOSTER,
QUI ES IN CEALIS
SANCTIFICETUR NOMEN TUUM

PATER NOSTER,
QUI ES IN CEALIS,
AMEN.

FATHER addresses the students.

FATHER: Please be seated. In the past week I have heard the most outrageous lies spreading throughout our school. I wish to remind you that God hears all and sees all and will not be tolerant of this type of behaviour. Weakness of character is the cause, lack of discipline. You can be better through the commitment to your faith; the Lord will keep us united and strong.

FATHER opens up to speak to all present.

We are all children of God.

Back to the students.

And without us you will be isolated and alone. Let us all remember the truth and continue to be guided by faith. Peace be with you, in holy and loving hearts.

ALL: *In nomine Patris, et Filii, et Spiritus Sancti. Amen.* (In the Name of the Father and of the Son and of the Holy Ghost. Amen.)

> *The children walk in a straight line and exit. Once FATHER CHRISTOPHER exits, JOANNA and ELIZABETH break off from the group and run to the field where JULIA is buried.*

JOANNA: You got it?

ELIZABETH: Yeah, they almost saw me jump the fence on my way back.

> *ELIZABETH pulls red flowers out of her pockets and hands one to JOANNA.*

BOTH: For Julia.

> *They place the flowers at their feet. SISTER BERNADETTE enters and watches the girls. The girls turn and are startled by SISTER; then they run off. FATHER CHRISTOPHER enters from the school and approaches SISTER BERNADETTE.*

FATHER: Sister Bernadette, I have been looking for you.

SISTER: Have you?

FATHER: You were not present at the chapel this morning. I realize you have had a number of hard weeks but regardless of these issues, we must set a good example for the children.

SISTER: A good example. I will do my best.

FATHER: You have taken an oath, Sister. I will count on you to be present from now on.

SISTER: Oh yes. I wouldn't miss it.

FATHER: I appreciate your support in this.

SISTER: By the book.

FATHER: Yes.

SISTER: The word of the Lord?

FATHER: Sister, is there something wrong?

SISTER: I'm fine. I was feeling ill this morning. Didn't have the energy…

FATHER: That is no excuse. We are to be the models of faith for these children.

SISTER: I didn't come because I cannot bear to look at you. Let alone all the children who are screaming for answers about Julia and all I can give them are lies! This is not the work I set out to do and you are certainly not the man I want to follow…

FATHER: Restrain yourself.

SISTER: Have we done our best? There isn't a shadow of a doubt that if we had let Julia run she would be alive today.

FATHER: You don't know that. We had no idea how she would respond.

SISTER: How was she supposed to respond to an act that the Bible clearly states as immoral?

FATHER: We did what had to be done. To protect the school, to ensure the work we do lives on.

SISTER: I know very well what you are capable of doing. I know what you have done and will continue to do.

FATHER: I do not know what you are implying.

SISTER: I saw it. I saw it with my own eyes.

FATHER: Sister, stop it, please. Shame on you, for suggesting such a thing. I pray that I will be able to forgive you for these accusations.

SISTER: Forgive me?

FATHER: And you must keep a better eye on your girls; clearly you have been too lenient in their discipline. Do what you have been taught to do.

FATHER CHRISTOPHER enters the school.

THEIR SPIRITS ARE BROKEN

SISTER BERNADETTE:
    I'VE ALWAYS BEEN TAUGHT:
    BE STRICT, BE STERN, BE RUTHLESS
    THEY SAID: NEVER GIVE IN,
    YOU MUST MAKE THEM UNDERSTAND
    BUT FATHER, I HAVE DOUBTS,
    I FEAR THAT IT'S BEEN USELESS
    AND FATHER, I'M AFRAID I LET IT GET OUT OF
    HAND.

    I PROMISED YOU, LORD, I WOULDN'T GIVE IN
    TO TEMPTATION
    I PROMISED MYSELF I'D GO OUT AND MAKE
    GOOD.
    YOUR GOODNESS HAS BEEN BLURRED,
    AND BROKEN IN YOUR IMAGE.
    YOUR GOODNESS IS WHAT'S LEFT ME
    TOO FAR FROM WHERE I STOOD.

    THEIR SPIRITS ARE BROKEN,
    DESPERATE, AND THEY'RE GRIEVING
    THEY WON'T EVER GO BACK
    TO THE WAY WE WERE BEFORE
    WE ARE NOT SAFE WITH FATHER HERE
    DECEIVING,
    I CAN'T BEAR THE THOUGHT OF BEING PART
    OF THIS ONCE MORE.

    FORGIVE WHAT I LACK
    THAT I TURNED MY BACK
    WHEN SHE CAME HERE
    I SENT HER TO PRAY,
    AND TURNED HER AWAY,
    IT'S ALL CLEAR.

    WITH NOWHERE TO GO
    WITH ALL THAT I KNOW
    ABANDON THIS FIGHT
    ABANDON MY LIGHT
    MY VOW

THERE WAS A TIME I HAD FAITH IN OUR
COUNTRY
I SAW ALL WE WERE DOING, BUT WHAT WE
ARE DOING IS WRONG.
WHO AM I NOW WHEN THE WORLD I KNOW'S
BEEN TAINTED
WHERE DO I GO WHEN THE WORLD I KNOW IS
GONE

> *All students circle SISTER BERNADETTE.
> She joins their circle.*

ALL STUDENTS:

AHHHH…
YAH HEY YAH WAY HEY YA HAH
AHHHH…
YAH HEY YAH WAY HEY YA HAH
AHHHH…
YAH HEY YAH WAY HEY YA HAH
AHHHH…

> *TOMMY emerges from the group and stands
> alone in the field. There is the loud sound of a
> train whistle.*

WONDERLAND

TOMMY:

WE DON'T NEED ANY FATHERS
WE DON'T NEED ANY MOTHERS
NOW THAT YOU'VE TAUGHT THE SAVAGE
WHAT WILL HE DO?

WAITS FOR YOUR GOD TO SAVE HER
THE MAN WE'RE ORDERED TO PRAY TO
SHE WAS A SISTER, A DAUGHTER,
YOUR IGNORANT CHILD

THIS AIN'T NO WONDERLAND I'M LIVING
AND I CAN'T UNDERSTAND IT ALL
IF THIS IS WONDERLAND I'M TRAPPED IN
THEN I HOPE I'LL SURVIVE THE FALL.

> *SISTER BERNADETTE enters holding Julia's bag.*

TOMMY: Sister, if you've come to take me back. I won't go.

SISTER: I have no intention of taking you back. I came to give you this.

> *She holds out Julia's backpack.*

TOMMY: Julia's?

SISTER: I thought you should have it. It's everything that was in her trunk. Take care, Tommy.

> *She gives the bag to TOMMY and starts to leave. He grabs it and hugs it tight.*

TOMMY: Sister, *Miigwetch*. (Thank you).

SISTER: And don't walk on the road until you're on the other side of town. After that point, they'll believe you when you say you aren't a runner from here.

> *SISTER BERNADETTE exits.*

TOMMY: YOU HAVE GUILT, WE HAVE SORROW
AFRAID OF THOSE WHO WE FOLLOW
THROUGH THESE DARKENED HALLS
THE PAIN SHINES THROUGH

THE SKY IS DARK, UNFORGIVING
IN THIS WORLD THAT WE'RE LIVING
MY FACE IS PLAGUED WITH THE SCARS
OF ALL IT HAS SEEN

THIS AIN'T NO WONDERLAND I'M LIVING
AND I CAN'T UNDERSTAND IT ALL
IF THIS IS WONDERLAND I'M TRAPPED IN
THEN I HOPE I'LL SURVIVE THE FALL.

> *Voices are heard off in the distance, as if they're calling to him from across the field.*

ALL CAST: *(Overlapping.)*
                THIS AIN'T NO WONDERLAND I'M LIVING
                AND I CAN'T UNDERSTAND IT ALL
                IF THIS IS WONDERLAND I'M TRAPPED IN
                THEN I HOPE I'LL SURVIVE THE FALL.

TOMMY, JULIA, RITA:
                (Overlapping.)
                THE FALL I'M LIVING
                AND I CAN'T UNDERSTAND IT ALL
                I'M TRAPPED IN
                THEN I HOPE I'LL SURVIVE THE FALL

Scene 6

> *Night still. TOM sits on RITA's porch, holding his father's red pouch.*

TOM: WHAT IF I NEEDED A FATHER
I COULD HAVE NEEDED A MOTHER
NOW WHAT'S LEFT IS THE MEMORY
NO ONE WILL KNOW.

> *RITA enters.*

RITA: It has tobacco in it. Your father gave it to me before he left. To keep you safe.

TOM: I don't think it worked.

RITA: When you first came home, I told you I thought I saw Julia in town a few times; she was walking on the road or into a building and I would always miss her. Always a few steps behind. All this time I've been dreaming of a new life for her, thinking that she was with some guy and had a family by now.

TOM: I was trying to save you from it. Four years old, Ma. Little kids. I remember you made us excited that we were going by train. It was a big deal back then, our first train ride, thinking we were off to some place with other kids just like us. It was such a long way, and we didn't know... I missed you so much; so every day, I went out to the edge of the field and waited, sometimes twice a day for the two o'clock train and even the seven, thinking that maybe you would be on that one. That maybe you'd be coming to take us home. *(Pause.)* And the years went by.

RITA: We came to get you and camped outside the school waiting to see you. One day the sheriff and priest came to us saying they would arrest us if we didn't leave. We didn't have a choice.

TOM: Julia...

AND WE WAIT

I've waited twenty years to tell you, but I would have waited my whole life to not have to see the way you're looking at me right now.

WHAT I WOULDN'T GIVE TO SEE
HER FACE, HER SMILE, HER EYES
EVERYTIME I SEE YOUR FACE
I SEE HER EYES

AND WE WAIT
AND WE WAIT

RITA: YOU ARE JUST LIKE YOUR FATHER
YOU SAVE ME THE PAIN WHILE YOU PULL AWAY

AND WE WAIT
AND WE WAIT

TOM: WHAT I WOULDN'T GIVE TO SEE
HER FACE, HER SMILE, HER EYES
EVERYTIME I SEE YOUR FACE I SEE HER EYES

BOTH: AND WE WAIT
AND WE WAIT

RITA: I know.

They hug.

TOM: They never even admitted to anything. And they just buried her in the dirt at the edge of the field as if she had never been.

RITA: We need to remember her now. Her spirit is still out there.

TOM: What are you talking about?

RITA: You said that they never had a ceremony to remember her – let's have our own.

TOM: That doesn't make it right.

RITA: It will help us honour her. We are going to visit her tonight.

TOM: What? Ma, I can't go back there…

RITA: Sure you can! Go on, grab your coat, it's chilly out here.

>   *RITA exit.*

TOM: Jesus Christ, Ma.

RITA: (*Offstage.*) Tom, move it!

>   *As TOM leaves, the students enter, circle him, and place red flowers all over taking us back to the field.*

ALL STUDENTS:
>   AHHHH…
>   YAH HEY YAH WAY HEY YA HAH
>   AHHHH…
>   YAH HEY YAH WAY HEY YA HAH
>   AHHHH…

>   *RITA enters and faces TOM. The sound of a train whistle is heard off in the distance. The students exit past RITA without noticing her.*

>   YAH HEY YAH WAY HEY YA HAH
>   AHHHH…

Scene 7

In the field outside the school, the sun is coming up on the horizon. Standing in the centre of the field is TOM, taking in the sky behind him.

RITA: I'm right behind you, Tom.

TOM: I promised myself I'd never come back here.

RITA: And here you are.

TOM: It's smaller than I remember. *(Pause.)* And this is where it happened...

RITA: Look at that sky. It has turned the brightest red.

TOM: Has it ever.

RITA: You are a good man, Tom. No matter all the shit they put in your head. I can still see my son in there. The sweet, gentle boy I let slip through my hands all those years ago. I can see him.

TOM: What do we do now?

RITA: I don't know, but I'll teach you a bit of what I remember. First, you hold the tobacco in your hands. We honour the four directions and her spirit in this place. Then put the tobacco down at your feet as an offering to the Creator. You don't need to rush when you put it down, but only think good thoughts. Then we sing her off. My *Nokomiss* (grandmother) used to tell me when we sing to the Creator we need to sing with all our voices so he can hear us and know she's coming and welcome her to the other side.

BAAMAAPII KA WAB MIGO
(until we see you again)

NI CHI CHAGNA,
WAY HEY YA HEY
WAY HEY YA HEY
YA HEY YA HEY YO

JULIA, KAH MEHZ NIGO (We'll miss you, Julia)
NGUY KAA WAA MIGO (We didn't say goodbye)
N'GII KITZEH MEH (We didn't get to say)
JIBWAA KEY JEHMAJAWYIN (Before you left us)

NONGWAA DUSH (And now)
KWI NEHMAW MAW MEH (We're going to pray)
GZMINDOO (Great Spirit)
WIIGA NOOHNAW MEH (We will call upon)

> *RITA teaches it to TOM and has him face the four directions to honour her spirit in this place. RITA faces each direction as she sings, TOM repeats after her.*

RITA: *ZHAW WHE NUNG* (South)

TOM: *ZHAW WHE NUNG* (South)

RITA: *WAA BAW NUNG* (East)

TOM: *WAA BAW NUNG* (East)

RITA: *KEY WED NONG EH PEH* (North)

TOM: *KEY WED NONG EH PEH* (North)

RITA: *EPIGIISH MOOK* (West)

TOM: *EPIGIISH MOOK* (West)

> *TOM steps forward, opens the red pouch, and places the tobacco down at his feet.*

RITA: *MNIDOOK* (Spirits)
NEHGII YEHNAW, JULIA (Take Julia home)
NOKOMISS MIINWAA MISHOOMISS
(Grandmother and Grandfather)
MUSSEH OOK (They're walking)
MNIDOOK (Spirits)
NEHGII YEHNAW, JULIA (Take Julia home)
KWII BEHNAWNAW MIK WAAKUNKING (They're coming to take you to the spirit world)

RITA: HI YEAH HI YEAH HI YAH YAH
            HI YEAH HI YEAH HI YAH YAH

> *TOM remembers the song and begins to sing under his breath.*

HI YEAH HI YEAH HI YAH YAH YAH
HI YEAH HI YEAH HI YAH

RITA & TOM: HI YEAH HI YEAH HI YAH YAH
             HI YEAH HI YEAH HI YAH YAH
             HI YEAH HI YEAH HI YAH YAH YAH
             HI YEAH HI YEAH HI YAH

> *JULIA appears from across the field and watches them from off in the distance.*

RITA, TOM, JULIA:
            HI YEAH HI YEAH HI YAH YAH
            HI YEAH HI YEAH HI YAH YAH
            HI YEAH HI YEAH HI YAH YAH YAH
            HI YEAH HI YEAH HI YAH

> *JULIA walks toward them. JULIA holds TOM's hand. RITA speeds up the drumming.*

HI YEAH HI YEAH HI YAH YAH
HI YEAH HI YEAH HI YAH YAH
HI YEAH HI YEAH HI YAH YAH YAH
HI YEAH HI YEAH HI YAH

> *The entire cast enters standing behind watching in witness to the ceremony.*

ALL: HI YEAH HI YEAH HI YAH YAH
            HI YEAH HI YEAH HI YAH YAH
            HI YEAH HI YEAH HI YAH YAH YAH
            HI YEAH HI YEAH HI YAH

> *All cast and musicians join the family holding hands, those on the ends step into the audience and hold an audience member's hand, completing the circle. This repeats many times until audience joins in song. After audience begins to*

sing, JULIA steps forward, turns to see everyone singing for her, honouring her, she smiles and makes her way through the audience. From a distance she looks back one last time. She exits.

RITA: *Baamaapii Ka Wab Migo, Julia.* (Until we see you again, Julia.)

TOM: Goodbye, Julia.

RITA drums one last time.

The End.

Children of God

Study Guide

Purpose of this Guide

This study guide is meant to serve as a companion piece to the play for students and educators.

It identifies key themes in hopes of increasing understanding of these topics, and to spark careful conversations about them. *Children of God* deals with some very serious issues, and discussions need to proceed with self-awareness and caution. As noted, residential schools cannot be talked about without recognizing the horrors that ensued: physical abuse, child rape, family separation, and cultural assimilation, to name but a few.

Many Aboriginal communities are still reeling from the impacts of residential school and are involved in ongoing processes of healing. It can be traumatic and draining for these communities to shoulder the sole burden of educating others about the histories of the residential school system. Educators thus have a unique opportunity, and indeed a responsibility, to teach young people about this history. Doing so will help foster a generation of students equipped with this knowledge, and hopefully encourage a generation of change-makers who will contribute to the work of healing from this dark legacy. This study guide hopes to serve as an entry point into these conversations.

This guide was written through reading the script, watching rehearsals, and talking with certain members of the cast and crew. It was written by a First Nations and Indigenous Studies major at the University of British Columbia, and was approached with an understanding of settler colonialism as an ongoing process that continues to this day. It was thus written with an understanding of youth and young scholars as carriers of change – as agents responsible for dismantling the structures that hold us down and keep us apart from each other.

Children of God touches on themes of shame, trauma, abuse, and settler colonialism. It is not within the scope of the study guide to study these major themes in-depth, but is instead meant to offer guidance in starting conversations around them.

Sol Diana, B.A.
Study Guide Author

Content Advisory and Self-Care

This play contains explicit descriptions and depictions of physical abuse, sexual abuse, and suicide. The play also deals with the history of residential schools in Canada. This is a recent history, as the last school did not close until 1996.

These topics can be distressing, traumatic, and / or triggering for members of the audience, especially those who have had first-hand experiences with these issues, or who know someone who has. With regard to residential school, some readers or audience members may have Elders or other family members who went to residential school, or even may have gone to residential school themselves.

Trauma is an overwhelming reaction to stressful and distressing situations. It can occur from a direct experience of trauma or from witnessing or listening to stories that are traumatic. Even if we don't experience a trauma reaction, it is important to acknowledge when a situation is overwhelming so that we can take care of ourselves.

The caring professions have found that witnessing trauma and becoming invested in overwhelming emotional stories can impact our health, well-being, and energy if we don't engage in self-care. Self-care is important after experiencing or witnessing a traumatic situation; it can help us reduce the stress of processing the event.

Some self-care strategies include:

- Exercising
- Getting adequate sleep
- Healthy eating
- Practicing mindfulness techniques such as meditation or yoga
- Speaking with a counsellor, or someone you trust

Our communities also play a role in our self-care. Having people around us that we trust to help us debrief, laugh, and give us comfort: these are important components of self-care. It is also possible that witnessing and understanding the injustices in our communities and societies can lead to overwhelming emotions. Self-care can also be found in taking action on the issues that are causing us stress. Working towards a better world can inspire hope within us when trauma events leave us feeling hopeless.

Resources

24-Hour National Survivors Crisis Line: 1-866-925-4419

How clinicians practice self-care: https://psychcentral.com/lib/how-clinicians-practice-self-care-9-tips-for-readers/

A list of resources on self-care for activists and people invested in social change: http://www.guerrillafeminism.org/guerrilla-feminist-digital-activist-resource-center/radical-self-care/

Special thanks to the UBC School of Social Work who kindly offered guidance in the writing of this section.

Residential Schools in Canada (Background)

The residential school system in Canada was designed to steal Aboriginal children from their home communities and force them to become more like Euro-Christian citizens of Canadian society. As former prime minister Stephen Harper's famous quotation from his 2008 apology to residential school survivors goes, the residential schools were meant "to kill the Indian in the child."

Set up by the federal government, and primarily run by the church, the residential schools sprawled across the nation throughout the 19th and 20th centuries. The last one did not close until 1996.

The system was rooted in the idea that European civilization was superior to the diverse civilizations of the Indigenous peoples, and that it was thus Canada's moral and God-given responsibility to save Aboriginal children from themselves. By isolating the children from their lands, their languages, their relations, and their traditions, and simultaneously immersing them in European customs, primarily rigid gender roles, Anglo mono-lingualism, and industrial vocational training, it was thought that Aboriginal communities would die out, and that a unified Canadian nation would emerge.

Residential schools, at their core, were built to commit what is called "cultural genocide." These schools often became places where children would do menial tasks designed to keep the schools open at low cost, rather than as sites of meaningful education. It is also widely reported that these schools were sites of brutal physical, emotional, and sexual abuse against the children, often as punishment for speaking their traditional language, or for trying to escape. Many children died while at these schools.

The Lasting Effects of Residential Schools

Children of God explores the horrible legacy of the residential school system that is still felt today by many Indigenous peoples.

Many of the youth who attended residential schools grew up learning to hate their culture, and many suffered physical and sexual abuse; this has had disastrous impacts for Indigenous communities. Many survivors of the schools grew into adulthood lacking parenting skills, fostering another generation of children without a nurturing family environment. In some communities today, rates of domestic abuse, alcoholism, and youth suicide are high. Observers have traced many of these issues back to the residential school system and the lack of self-esteem it instilled in the students. This ongoing process of undermining community well-being and cohesion, despite the fact that the schools have been closed, is often referred to as intergenerational trauma.

Healing from Residential Schools

While understanding the vile history of residential schools and the lingering ramifications of this system, it is also important to pause and recognize that this trauma does not define Indigenous peoples and their communities. Many First Nations communities today are healthy and thriving, have a strong connection to their lands and traditions, and are raising younger generations that are eager and ready to continue this process.

On a national scale, it is becoming more common to talk about the residential schools in an honest way for Indigenous and non-Indigenous peoples alike – partly thanks to the Truth and Reconciliation Commission, which sought to offer space and a platform for survivors of the schools to talk about their experiences as a means of mending relations between Canada and Indigenous nations. Reconciliation politics is by no means perfect, and many First Nations are waiting for the federal government to deliver on its promise of better futures, but we now have valuable entry points into necessary conversations around what healing can look like.

Many communities that still experience the lingering impact of residential schools are taking matters into their own hands, and are looking to break cycles of intergenerational trauma through their own community-led initiatives, such as education, residential school survivor–oriented societies, and drug and alcohol intervention programs.

The Truth and Reconciliation Commission Findings

http://www.trc.ca/websites/trcinstitution/index.php?p=890

Resources on Healing and Healing Initiatives

Aboriginal Healing Foundation:
http://www.ahf.ca/

Legacy of Hope:
http://legacyofhope.ca/

The Indian Residential School Survivors Society:
http://www.irsss.ca/

Where Are the Children? Healing the Legacy of the Residential Schools:
http://wherearethechildren.ca/

Key Terms Glossary

ABORIGINAL
The first peoples of Canada, including First Nations, Metis, and Inuit peoples. It became a popular term after 1982, when Section 35 of the Canadian Constitution defined "Aboriginal" in this way.

FIRST NATIONS
The Aboriginal peoples of Canada (excluding Metis and Inuit). It does not have a legal definition, but it has been popular practice since the 1970s to use "First Nations" in replacement of the term "Indian," as many have begun to perceive "Indian" to be derogatory. According to Indigenous Foundations (2009), an online UBC-run resource, the singular "First Nation" can refer to "a band, a reserve-based community, or a larger tribal grouping and the status Indians who live in them. For example, the Stó:lō Nation (which consists of several bands), or the Tsleil-Waututh Nation (formerly the Burrard Band)."

INDIAN
A legal term that refers to a First Nations person who is registered as such under the *Indian Act*. It is best practice to only use the term "Indian" in this context, as many people since the 1970s have begun to believe the term to be offensive and outdated. *Children of God* takes place during a time when it is still a popular term, and uses it extensively.

INDIAN ACT
A Canadian federal law meant to govern Aboriginal life. Since its beginnings, it has been highly invasive and controlling. According to Indigenous Foundations (2009):

> This authority has ranged from overarching political control, such as imposing governing structures on Aboriginal communities in the form of band councils, to control over the rights of Indians to practice their culture and traditions. The

Indian Act has also enabled the government to determine the land base of these groups in the form of reserves, and even to define who qualifies as Indian in the form of Indian status.

It was the *Indian Act* that, in the 1920s, made it mandatory for every child with Indian status to attend residential school.

INDIGENOUS

A term that encompasses a wide range of Aboriginal peoples, and is typically used in international contexts (most notably the United Nations). This study guide uses this term extensively to refer to Aboriginal peoples in Canada.

RESIDENTIAL SCHOOL

Indigenous Foundations (2009) defines the term as:

> an extensive school system set up by the Canadian government and administered by churches that had the nominal objective of educating Aboriginal children but also the more damaging and equally explicit objectives of indoctrinating them into Euro-Canadian and Christian ways of living and assimilating them into mainstream Canadian society.

The residential schools were, at their core, meant to undermine Aboriginal communities by taking the children away and making them Euro-Canadian.

Children of God takes place during the 1950s and 1970s, and is set during a time when it is mandatory by law for all Indian children to attend residential school.

SETTLER COLONIALISM AND ASSIMILATION

Settler colonialism is the ongoing process of destroying one society for the purpose of replacing it with another one. To justify this, the Indigenous peoples need to be perceived as inferior in contrast to the colonizing group, and thus deserving of what happens to them.

Canada is founded on settler colonialism, and this process of erasure was done first through force – outright genocide – and then later through more subtle strategies of containment, such as law (the *Indian Act*).

Children of God takes place during this shift from force to "soft power" rule over Aboriginal communities. The residential school system, though seemingly less violent than genocide, had the same goal. It was thought that training Indian children to be Canadian when they were young would eventually bring about the slow death of Aboriginal communities, and that this mass death would open up more land for Canadian nation-building. This slow process is also known as assimilation – stripping a group of people of their identities and then absorbing them into a mainstream culture.

Settler colonialism is still happening today, though it is getting more and more tricky to pinpoint exactly how. Many critics point out that the *Indian Act*, though it has been amended many times since its inception, has largely maintained its original form. It is still designed to govern and control First Nations communities, as well as to give Canada access to their lands, most notably for energy projects.

Also, the structure of the residential schools remains today in the form of Canada's foster care system. Remember that the residential school system would take children away from communities the federal government deemed "unsafe." Today, the government continues to take children away from their communities, placing them in foster care. This process began in the 1960s, and has been called by the chilling term "The Sixties Scoop." It has been calculated that there are more Aboriginal children in foster care today than there were children in the residential schools (The Canadian Press 2011).

Key Themes and Discussion Questions

Children of God masterfully navigates complex and sensitive issues. This section identifies three of these core interrelated themes, as well as accompanying questions meant to spark further discussion in small groups.

1. Remembrance

Time and memory play central roles in *Children of God*. When siblings Tommy and Julia are in residential school in the 1950s, memory of life before they came to the school is beautifully explored. Consider Scene 6 of Act 1, where the boys are writing their mandatory letters home. After Father Christopher sends Wilson and Vincent back to their dorms but keeps Tommy back to continue writing his letter, the song "Who I Was" begins. Tommy, instead of adhering to the template written on the board, decides to write a personalized letter in his own language, and to secretly send it to the chief of his community. This act marks a return to a past self that he was taught to abandon, as he sings,

> *For the first time it's not an image*
> *For the first time it's not a sound*
> *For the first time it's a real memory*
> *Quick before it's gone, write it down*
> *This is the start of what I remember*
> *This is the start of what I lost*
> *This is the start of what Ma told us*
> *Maybe this is who I was*

Here, remembering is a form of resistance. If the intent of the residential schools was to "kill the Indian in the child," Tommy remembering life before residential school powerfully indicates that the system has momentarily failed.

Discussion Questions:

- Brainstorm with a partner or with a small group other moments where time and memory play an important role in *Children of God.*

- Can you think of a time when a memory brought you strength or comfort?

2. Shame

The impact of the residential schools on the children who attended is powerfully and vividly explored in *Children of God,* particularly in showing the shame that the children were taught to feel about themselves. For example, when Tom applies to work with Wilson's company twenty years after they were classmates at the residential school, there is a stigma and an embarrassment around acting "Indian" when in "professional"(in Western standards) settings. This can be seen most clearly when Wilson and Tom meet for a drink and Tom angrily says to Wilson, "You tell me to come to a dive bar so your work friends don't see you talking to an Indian. This act has done good for you, huh? Pretending to be a white man, forgetting where you came from. You're the whitewashing they wanted us to be."

"They," here, evidently refers to the residential school system, and Tom's accusation paints a troubling, yet clear picture of the racism that undergirds the system's operation, and how it has impacted the boys differently. Here, Wilson has apparently internalized the shame of being Native to the extent that he has sought to reinvent himself as a White Canadian, which has benefited him. Tom, however, is still clutching to his Indigeneity, and continues to be punished for it. Although Tom and Wilson are no longer students in the school, the intent of "killing the Indian in the child" is still at play – a powerful reminder of the lasting effects of shame.

Shame plays out in *Children of God* in other moments as well, such as Vincent's and Julia's suicides, and Julia's unexpected pregnancy – of which Father Christopher explains, "An Indian girl with a child will be damned to hell."

In all of these cases, *Children of God* seems to be emphasizing to the audience how the residential school system prevented the growth of First Nations communities. The schools were places that led children to take their own lives, and where the possibility of a newborn child is considered to be a sin.

Discussion Questions:

- With a partner or in small groups, identify other moments in the play where the impacts of residential school were portrayed or referenced. Why were these depictions important?

- When you are feeling down or embarrassed, what is something you do, or can do, to deal with these feelings? What makes you feel powerful?

3. Agency and Resistance

Director and writer Corey Payette does a wonderful job balancing honest portrayals of the horror of the residential schools with moments of happiness and love. *Children of God* is careful to not depict the atrocities of the residential schools as the defining experience for the children, and shows the audience that the children have agency.

Agency, sometimes called *autonomy*, means that a person has the power to act how they wish in a given environment, and that they have control over their bodies, behaviour, and emotions. Because residential schools were designed to turn children into Euro-Christian citizens, acts of agency (like remembrance) represent acts of resistance.

Children of God is filled with moments where the characters enact various forms of resistance in the face of strict rules and punishments at the school. Notable examples include Julia's repeated escape attempts; the children's visit to Julia when she is locked in the cellar and the eating of stolen food together; Tommy's attempts to write a letter to his hometown's chief in his own language; the boys' secret mocking of Father Christopher; Julia and Tommy's conversations in Ojibway; the children's turning of their picnic blanket into a drum; and Elizabeth's picking of red flowers to mourn Julia's death.

All of these examples remind the audience that despite the

horrors they are facing, the children are ultimately humans, and they hold power to act for themselves.

Discussion Questions:

- Do you think wanting to escape the school represents a sign of strength, or weakness, for the children?
- With a partner or in small groups, reflect on a moment where you stood up for yourself or others. What inspired you to act?
- With a partner or in small groups, share something unique about you. What makes you *you*?

Further Discussion Questions

- How many of these key terms were you already familiar with? How did you learn them?
- Reflect on the title of the play, *Children of God*. What images or immediate thoughts come to mind?
- If settler colonialism is about replacing one society with another, can you identify any ways in which this process is still happening today? Discuss with a partner or in small groups.
- With a partner or in small groups, brainstorm any other key themes from the play that you identify as important. Why are they important?
- *Children of God* takes place over sixty years ago, and the last residential school closed in 1996, over twenty years ago. Why is it so important to keep talking about them?
- Given what you know now, why is a play like *Children of God* so important?
- How will you tell others, such as your family, about this play? What are important points you think others should know?

Supplemental Activities

Be a Promoter!

- By yourself or in a group, design a promotional poster for *Children of God*. How will you illustrate the most important themes of the play?

Get in touch

- Write a letter to your favourite character from *Children of God*. What will you ask? How do you think they will respond?

"I Am" Poem and River Journey

- *Children of God* shows us the power of knowing who we are, and where we come from. Write an "I am" poem by listing off twenty distinctive things about yourself. It could be simple like "I am from Vietnam," or something even more detailed like, "I am a person who connects with my ancestors through eating what they used to eat."

- With these twenty things as a roadmap, draw a river that leads to where you are currently at in your life. Where does the river begin – when you were born? A thousand years ago? Yesterday? Where does the river flow through? What is the shape of the river – a spiral? A straight line? What surrounds the river – grass and rocks? Your family? Memories? Your worst fears? Your dreams?

Share your poem and river journey with others. The more people involved in this activity the better!

Sources

Van Dernoot Lipsky, L. (2009). *Trauma Stewardship: An Everyday Guide to Caring for Self While Caring for Others.* San Francisco: Berrett-Koehler Publishers.

Reynolds, V. (2011). "Supervision of solidarity practices: Solidarity teams and people-ing-the-room." *Context.* Pp. 4-7.

Reynolds, V. (2011). "Resisting burnout with justice-doing." *International Journal of Narrative Therapy & Community Work,* 4, pp. 27-45.

Crisis Centre. (2013). *Coping and Self-Care.* Retrieved from: https://crisiscentre.bc.ca/coping-and-self-care/

Hanson, Erin. "The Residential School System." *UBC Indigenous Foundations.* Web. 2017. http://indigenousfoundations.adm.arts.ubc.ca/the_residential_school_system/

Hanson, Erin. "The Residential School System." *UBC Indigenous Foundations.* Web. 2009. http://indigenousfoundations.adm.arts.ubc.ca/the_residential_school_system/

"Terminology." UBC *Indigenous Foundations.* Web. 2009. http://indigenousfoundations.adm.arts.ubc.ca/terminology/

The Canadian Press. "First Nations Children Still Taken from Parents." *CBCnews.* CBC/Radio Canada, 02 Aug. 2011. Web. http://www.cbc.ca/news/politics/first-nations-children-still-taken-from-parents-1.1065255

"The Indian Act." *UBC Indigenous Foundations.* Web. 2009. http://indigenousfoundations.adm.arts.ubc.ca/the_indian_act/